Psychoanalytic Co.

Psychoanalytic Complexity is the application of a multidisciplinary, explanatory theory to clinical psychoanalysis and psychotherapy. It offers a framework with which to understand the origins and perpetuation of emotional distress and associated painful relationship experiences, and a practical mode of transforming this framework into a clinical sensibility (or a specific array of clinical attitudes) that will advance clinicians' work and more effectively bring about therapeutic change. William J. Coburn presents a revolutionary and far-reaching counterpoint to the remnants of Cartesianism and scientism, respecting and encouraging human anomaly rather than pathologizing or obliterating the uniqueness of the individual.

In *Psychoanalytic Complexity*, William J. Coburn explores the value of complexity theory as an explanatory framework with which clinicians can better understand, retrospectively, therapeutic action and the change process. He further extends this sensibility by examining the ways in which such a theoretical framework can inform what clinicians can do, prospectively, to effect positive change within the therapeutic relationship. He persuasively argues that the medium of bringing to light new ways of relating, emotional experiencing, and meaning making resides in the fundamental attitudes derived from a complexity theory sensibility as applied to psychoanalysis and psychotherapy.

Using a variety of clinical illustrations throughout, *Psychoanalytic Complexity* is a radical corrective to reductionism and the more traditional presumption that the problems in analysis lie with the patient and that the cure lies with the therapist. It offers a new language, vocabulary, and way of thinking, and a new way of being with others that is key in arriving at affirmative therapeutic change. This book is intended for psychoanalysts, clinical psychologists, therapists, mental health counselors, academics, and teachers who are interested in new trends in psychoanalysis and psychotherapy.

William J. Coburn is a psychoanalyst and licensed clinical psychologist in Los Angeles. He is joint editor-in-chief of the *International Journal of Psychoanalytic Self Psychology* and senior faculty member and training and supervising analyst at the Institute of Contemporary Psychoanalysis in Los Angeles. He co-edited (with Roger Frie) *Persons In Context: The Challenge of Individuality in Theory and Practice* (2011, Routledge).

PSYCHOANALYTIC INQUIRY BOOK SERIES
JOSEPH D. LICHTENBERG
SERIES EDITOR

Like its counterpart, *Psychoanalytic Inquiry: A Topical Journal for Mental Health Professionals*, the Psychoanalytic Inquiry Book Series presents a diversity of subjects within a diversity of approaches to those subjects. Under the editorship of Joseph Lichtenberg, in collaboration with Melvin Bornstein and the editorial board of *Psychoanalytic Inquiry*, the volumes in this series strike a balance between research, theory, and clinical application. We are honored to have published the works of various innovators in psychoanalysis, such as Frank Lachmann, James Fosshage, Robert Stolorow, Donna Orange, Louis Sander, Léon Wurmser, James Grotstein, Joseph Jones, Doris Brothers, Fredric Busch, and Joseph Lichtenberg, among others.

The series includes books and monographs on mainline psychoanalytic topics, such as sexuality, narcissism, trauma, homosexuality, jealousy, envy, and varied aspects of analytic process and technique. In our efforts to broaden the field of analytic interest, the series has incorporated and embraced innovative discoveries in infant research, self psychology, intersubjectivity, motivational systems, affects as process, responses to cancer, borderline states, contextualism, postmodernism, attachment research and theory, medication, and mentalization. As further investigations in psychoanalysis come to fruition, we seek to present them in readable, easily comprehensible writing.

After 25 years, the core vision of this series remains the investigation, analysis and discussion of developments on the cutting edge of the psychoanalytic field, inspired by a boundless spirit of inquiry.

PSYCHOANALYTIC INQUIRY BOOK SERIES
JOSEPH D. LICHTENBERG
SERIES EDITOR

PSYCHOANALYTIC INQUIRY BOOK SERIES
JOSEPH D. LICHTENBERG
SERIES EDITOR

PSYCHOANALYTIC INQUIRY BOOK SERIES
JOSEPH D. LICHTENBERG
SERIES EDITOR

Psychoanalytic Complexity

Clinical Attitudes for Therapeutic Change

William J. Coburn

Routledge
Taylor & Francis Group

NEW YORK AND LONDON

First published 2014
by Routledge
711 Third Avenue, New York, NY 10017

and by Routledge
27 Church Road, Hove, East Sussex BN3 2FA

Routledge is an imprint of the Taylor & Francis Group, an informa business

© 2014 Taylor & Francis

The right of William J. Coburn to be identified as author of this work
has been asserted by him in accordance with sections 77 and 78 of the
Copyright, Designs and Patents Act 1988.

Library of Congress Cataloging in Publication Data
Coburn, William J.
Psychoanalytic complexity : clinical attitudes for therapeutic change /
William J. Coburn.
      pages cm. – (Psychoanalytic inquiry book series ; no. 42)
      1. Psychotherapy – Philosophy. 2. Psychoanalysis. 3. Therapist and
      patient. I. Title.
      RC437.5.C63 2014
      616.89′14–dc23   2013024904
ISBN: 978-0-415-89623-8 (hbk)
ISBN: 978-0-415-89624-5 (pbk)
ISBN: 978-1-315-85668-1 (ebk)

Typeset in Times
by HWA Text and Data Management, London

To my father, who I wish were present, and to my son, who perpetually inspires me.

Contents

Preface

One shouldn't complicate things for the pleasure of complicating, but one should also never simplify or pretend to be sure of such simplicity where there is none. If things were simple, word would have gotten around.

—Jacques Derrida[1]

Around the time of Ferenczi Sandor, a novel by Ferenc Molnar emerged from within 1906 Budapest culture and was considered generally a good read by young people everywhere, especially as it reflected, through metaphor, a scathing satirical portrayal of European nationalism and a rather accurate premonition of the First World War. Titled *A Pal Utcai Fiuk*, or *The Paul Street Boys*, the story revolved around a gang of street kids who fervently defend their playground against another gang of kids who wish to invade their territory. The Paul Street Boys are especially known for their routinely passing around a wad of gum, called *gitt*, which was essentially window putty. Yum. Here in the United States, we as kids used to call this ABC (already been chewed) gum. In grand street style known only to adolescents, these boys would surreptitiously scrape and collect the coveted putty that held home windows in place and render it into a chewing gum worthy of a convenience store shelf. This one wad of gum united the *Gittegylet*— the boys who chew the same wad—far more adhesively than it did the windows it had held in place. Among popular agreement, the *gitt* would thus be passed around, after a predetermined time period, from one boy to the next, effectively affording each an opportunity to savor this delectable chaw while also keeping it moist, and alive. It is not lost on me that a similar phenomenon exists in our psychoanalytic and psychotherapy communities, wherein the perhaps over-valued putty is replaced with theories and variations on theories. And in many respects, with a few notable exceptions, the enjoyment of passing around the same chaw, uniting us and perhaps placing one's own indentation on it before the expectable and anticipated handing it over is consummated, is exactly how we spend much of our time. Whether the contents of this book will be yet another and familiar piece of *gitt* or perhaps a new, freshly scraped piece of putty to share only you can decide for yourself. For me, it does have a fresh taste, but perhaps it is still putty nevertheless. At the very least, if you enjoy chewing it for a while, I will feel some sense of accomplishment.

This book, in large part, is a thought experiment, one in which I invite you to consider some rather revolutionary ideas, to immerse yourself in a new worldview, and then to see what happens next. I wish I could say these are my ideas, but they don't belong to anyone really. No one invented complexity theory. Rather, it emerged over the last century predominantly through the independent theorizing of mathematicians, biologists, physicists, astronomers, meteorologists, economists, and those who are obsessed with the study of slime mold. It has wound its way into computer science and the arts. Complexity theory, in the broad sense of the term, reflects the perpetual and continuous thought and imagination of many individuals from diverse professional backgrounds and cultures.

After a while, some folks began to realize that scientist-explorers from diverse fields were independently developing uncannily similar ideas about how their respective subjects of investigation—that is, systems such as molecules, cells, human bodies, families, cultures, solar systems, and so forth—work. And over time, a body of presumed knowledge about the behavior and characteristics of alive, vibrant, open systems emerged. As it turns out, molecular systems have a lot in common with meteorological systems, biological systems with economic systems, neurological systems with slime mold systems. This body of knowledge itself began to exhibit one of the very characteristics with which it was concerned: the property of emergence. And thus, over the last forty years or so, nonlinear dynamic systems theory—or complexity theory for short—coalesced as a field in its own right: the study of nonlinear, dynamic, complex systems of any ilk. In this sense, complexity theory, in addition to being considered multidisciplinary and cross-disciplinary, is now considered a transdisciplinary field (Krakauer 2009) aimed at investigating a wide and colorful range of interpenetrating systems of which each of us is a product and property. And if complexity theorists have learned nothing else over the years, they have at least come to understand that all things, including we humans, are inextricably connected in one way or another. This makes for a rather revolutionary, if unsettling, perspective on who we are and how the world works.

A variety of systems theories (Bateson 1942; Mead 1942; von Foerster 1981; Wiener 1948) was introduced into family therapy theory in the 1940s, but many of those perspectives still contained elements of a more traditional, objectivist worldview (for instance, the concept of homeostasis or the notion that one could step outside a particular system for the purposes of observation). From a more contemporary complexity sensibility, these concepts are no longer tenable. The appearance of homeostasis, for example, is now more profitably understood as the presence of one among many potential attractor states, or potential and identifiable configurations of the elements of a system. And there is no stepping outside a particular system for observation purposes—we can never disengage ourselves from the systems in which we remain relentlessly embedded (von Foerster 1981). By the 1970s, dynamic systems theorists had accrued more presumed knowledge about how open systems work, and a few psychologists and psychoanalysts began playing with the application of dynamic systems theory to their respective domains. In psychoanalysis, Robert Galatzer-Levy (1978) published his ground-breaking article, "Qualitative Change from Quantitative Change: Mathematical Catastrophe Theory in Relation to Psychoanalysis." However, perhaps because it was highly mathematical, this perspective was not easily accessible or readily amenable to translation into clinical application. Following Galatzer-Levy, several psychoanalysts, similarly intrigued with dynamic systems theory, jumped into what would become the complexity fray of the late 1990s. These included Hinshelwood (1982), Moran (1991), Sander (1988), Sashin and Callahan (1990), Spruiell (1993), Seligman and Shanok (1995), and Thelen and Smith (1994), just to name a few. Dynamic systems theory, however, enjoyed a substantial spike in interest after the publication of Thelen and Smith's seminal 1994 book on the application of nonlinear dynamic systems theory to developmental psychology. Their contemporary research findings on early human development overturned many of our assumptions about the epigenesis and teleology of early human life. We and the world we inhabit no longer seemed so stable and predictable, so fixed and accountable. And this has been very much to our advantage.

My own foray into, and passion for, complexity theory was ignited after my reading Robert Stolorow's influential 1997 article titled "Dynamic, dyadic, intersubjective systems: An evolving paradigm for psychoanalysis." Already fairly steeped in intersubjective systems theory, a radical phenomenological contextualist perspective (Stolorow, Atwood, and Orange 1998, 2002), I found this new complexity sensibility to be a rich and elucidating expansion of the contextualist spirit I had been fortunate to unearth previously in the work of the intersubjective systems theorists. It was in that year, 1997, that I sensed the potential impact a further examination and exploration of complexity might have on how we conceptualize the psychoanalytic and psychotherapeutic process. I felt like a kid in a sandbox already advantaged with lots of great toys, and now there was a new one, a powerful one, suddenly introduced into my play space. And yes, my subsequent efforts at insinuating complexity theory into psychoanalysis and psychotherapy have been predominantly just that: play. And, my own personal organizing principles notwithstanding, I have not been alone. A variety of additional theorists, many from my own institute—the Institute of Contemporary Psychoanalysis in Los Angeles—were playing as well [Bacal and Herzog (2003); Beebe et al. (2003); Beebe and Lachmann (2001); Bonn (2010); Charles (2002); Dubois (2003); Ghent (2002); Harris (2005); Lichtenberg, Lachmann, and Fosshage (1992); Magid (2002); Miller (1999); Orange (2006); Palombo (1999); Pickles (2006); Piers (2005); Sander (2002); Scharff (2000); Seligman (2005); Shane and Coburn (2002); Shane, Shane and Gales (1997); Sperry (2011); Steinberg (2006); Sucharov (2002); Thelen (2005); Trop, Burke and Trop (2002); VanDerHeide, (2009); Varela, Thompson and Rosch (1991); and Weisel-Barth (2006)]. Very exciting times, indeed!

As will be discussed shortly in more detail, complexity theory has been employed primarily for the purposes of trying to explain and account for the underlying fluidity, dynamism, and unpredictability of human systems, of trying to understand how things really work. It has been essentially a descriptive tool, a device for retrospective explanation. Why did that patient change in the way he did and in the specific time frame in which the change emerged? For understanding the emergence of emotional life and meaning, for grasping the intensely contextualized nature of human experiencing and existence, complexity theory offers a powerful explanatory framework, but a vital question follows: In what way might this sensibility shape our understanding of our patients *prospectively*, inform what we might do in the present and the future for our patients?[2] This book reflects the beginning stages of addressing this question and does so through the lens of examining the influential role our implicit and explicit attitudes play in the clinical surround.

Notes

1 Derrida, Jacques (1988) *Limited Inc.,* trans. S. Weber and J. Mehlman. Evanston, IL: Northwestern University Press, p. 119. English translation copyright © 1988 by Northwestern University Press. All rights reserved.
2 I am indebted to Estelle Shane for initially and relentlessly posing this question to me.

Acknowledgments

The pages that follow reflect certain facets of what I have learned about complexity over the last fifteen years or so, the results of my playing with exciting and inspiring ideas. And it reflects my initial steps in exploring how these ideas are useful clinically. For me, they have been life-altering and personally transformative. For all of this play, I owe an enormous debt of gratitude to a variety of people who have inspired me, taught me, and cared for me throughout this process. I thank Estelle Shane who, in innumerable ways, including closely reading and editing this book, has supported and guided me for many years and throughout this project. I am also deeply grateful to Robert Stolorow for his relentless care, attention, and support these last eighteen years, without whom this book would not have been possible. So much of writing, the exhilarating and arduous task of thinking and creating, necessitates a true sense of ownership of oneself, while also a sustained sense of connection with important others in one's life. Without Robert Stolorow, this also would not have been possible for me. I also thank wholeheartedly Jim Fosshage, whose friendship and guidance remain invaluable to me, as does the ever-present support of Joe Lichtenberg, whose passion and vision for creativity and writing have played an enormous role for me in the writing of this book. I am also indebted to Roger Frie, in whom I have found an invaluable friend and partner in thinking, creating, and publishing. I also thank other vital individuals who have always supported me and who have heavily influenced my work. They are Donna Orange, Lewis Aron, Howard Bacal, Arthur Malin, Marian Tolpin, Steven Stern, Paul Cilliers, Mark Taylor, Jill Gentile, Malcolm Slavin, Nancy VanDerHeide, Shelley Doctors, Lestor Lenoff, Frank Lachmann, Suzanne Lachmann, Lucyann Carlton, Margy Sperry, Peter Radestock, Richard Siegel, Hazel Ipp, Hannah Maizes, Nancy Goldman, Jeff Trop, Leonard Bearne, Kate Bracaglia, Kristopher Spring, Kristen Leishman, and Jackie Legg. Each person, in his or her own unique way, has inspired me immensely. I am also deeply grateful for the tireless support of my family, including Katalin, William, Alicia, Andy, Laura, Theodore, Jake, Todd, Linda, Nora, Morgan, Alex, Cassie, Ted, Mark, and Peggy. I also thank Markiss, Nacho, Kells, David, and Steve of the playa, whose spirit and support never fail to nurture me. Kate Hawes and Kirsten Buchanan at Routledge have given me invaluable support and guidance throughout the production phase of this book, for which I am deeply grateful. I also thank Rebekka Helford, who was immensely helpful, patient, kind, tireless, and supportive in the editing and preparation of this book.

Portions of the Introduction were first published in *Psychoanalytic Dialogues* (2011b, 21:128–139) and then substantially revised for purposes of this book. Segments of Chapter 1 of this volume are revised portions of text first published in *Psychoanalytic Inquiry* (2002, 22:5) and in Buirski and Kottler's *New Developments in Self Psychology Practice* (2007). Chapter 2 incorporates revised segments first published in *Psychoanalytic Dialogues* (2011b, 21:1) and (2012, 22:3). Portions of Chapter 3 were first published in the *Journal of the American Academy of Psychoanalysis* (1999, 26:2) and then heavily revised for inclusion in this book. Chapter 4 incorporates substantially revised segments of material first published in Frie and Orange's *Beyond Postmodernism: New Dimensions in Clinical Theory and Practice* (2009); in Buirski and Kottler's *New Developments in Self Psychology Practice* (2007); and in *Psychoanalytic Inquiry* (2002, 22:5). Segments of Chapter 5 were first published in Frie and Orange's *Beyond Postmodernism: New Dimensions in Clinical Theory and Practice* (2009) and then substantially revised for inclusion in this book. I thank the editors and publishers of these books and journals for granting me permission to incorporate this material in my book.

Introduction

Psychoanalytic Complexity: It's (Almost) All About Attitude

People out of each tradition are too religiously devoted to their particular theories to be able to sit back and say what are the assumptions here?
—Stephen Mitchell[1]

One way to evaluate a psychoanalytic theory is to picture a therapist with that theory in his mind and imagine what happens when we fold him into the basic soup of psychoanalytic procedure.
—Lawrence Friedman[2]

By the time you've read about halfway through this sentence (right about here), you already will have irrevocably and irreversibly stepped into a new complex system. (And, of course, you bring your socio-cultural-historically-derived attitudes with you.) Think of listening to the first phone message of a new patient: The moment you begin to register his voice—the content, the nuances of tone and rhythm, and so forth—you've already entered and helped to constitute a new, complex, relational system, altering something of your experiential world and, of course, something of his as well.

How have you already altered *his*? Your outgoing phone message, which he heard, whether he was really conscious of it or was not, was so highly specific in content, timing, rhythm, tone, and so forth and already contextualized by your own history, your own present emotional life, your imagined future, and innumerable other factors, that experiences and meanings are already being formed for him. And then: How soon will you return his call? Time matters in complex systems, as they move inexorably forward in time. What will your tone of voice be? Nuance matters, too. Initial conditions matter as well (Poincaré & Guillaume 1900). Not unlike what often accompanies the beginning of a new relationship, similarly, questions emerge about what it would mean to delve into the following pages, to commence a new adventure: Will this be helpful to me, will it change me, will it alter my emotional and clinical sensibility? What do I want from you, expect from you, and what do you want from this book, from me? To paraphrase Dickens, perhaps these pages will show.

We all want to know what works in psychoanalysis and psychotherapy and, of course, what doesn't. When I think about our contemporary ideas of therapeutic action and the change process, I am reminded of early man at the nighttime communal fire, reenacting for his clan his late-afternoon killing of a saber-tooth tiger. He plunges his spear into the ground with ferocity, twisting it from side to side, exciting sparks from the fire, as the tribe members look on with awe and reverence, even though the tiger may actually have fallen accidentally on this hunter's stick as he, the hunter, terrified, was attempting a hasty escape from certain death. After things turn out well, and the dust settles, and our heartbeats return to normal, we construct good, coherent stories about how and why things worked out, and usually these are not mystery stories about accidents and perplexity. Rather, we tend to graft what sounds like insight and good sense onto good outcomes and even sometimes insight and good sense onto bad outcomes. Naturally, we want to make sense of things and to have a say in how things turn out. This speaks to our incessant and necessary proclivity toward organization and explanation—speculating, theorizing, hypothesizing, abstracting, presuming, assuming, and generally trying to understand the world and our place within it. This is just what we do.

A principal avenue toward making sense of things is story and storytelling (Brooks 1994). Many of us love good stories, perhaps especially clinical ones, where, for a brief time, we can experience vicariously or perhaps watch dispassionately what someone else does, how someone else heals, or even how someone else gets into hot water with her patient. Despite our continued longing for and infatuation with new theories, it seems the mainstay of psychoanalytic writing remains a good story, one in which we eagerly witness through a kind of keyhole the struggles and the (familiar and occasionally disingenuous) happy outcomes. This is partly because we hope to glimpse something that might work next time with our patients, what it might look like to interpret or to enact and to live through adversity. Naturally, we want to know what works, because so often the currency of our clinical lives is mystery, uncertainty, and perplexity. And presumably we are not just in it for the adventure of it all—though that is an intriguing factor for many of us. Primarily, we want to effect useful change while, much like living with the inevitable fly in the ointment, simultaneously tolerating confusion and the unknown.

The obsession with statistically derived, *evidence-based* treatment in some sectors of the mental health field—which frequently includes normative presumptions about the nature of mental health, devoid of any consideration for the socio-cultural-historical-contextual origins from which they derive (Cushman 1994; Frie 2003, 2011; Masler forthcoming)—is a substantial instance of our discomfort with ambiguity and uncertainty (Brothers 2002) and our unwillingness to hold our theories, including our conclusions about truth and reality, lightly (Orange 1995). There are many other familiar instances of our human proclivity to systematize, codify, and standardize, yielding universal approaches to curing the psychopathology that we, culturally constituted ourselves, have otherwise only constructed. An aspect of the more extreme caricature of this brand of epistemological yearning is reflected in the *Just tell me what to do—I don't want to have to think about it myself* sensibility. As contemporary psychoanalysts and psychotherapists, we hope to eschew any notions and approaches that slide into reductionism and that universalize what can only be discovered, witnessed, and experienced on an individual-by-individual, system-by-system basis.

As contextualists and systems thinkers, however, we are always concerned with how we define useful change, on a person-by-person basis, and how we think about effecting such change. Hence, we think about not just what might cause change (therapeutic action) but also what kind of change we want to realize. Psychoanalysis and psychotherapy should be as much about defining what needs changing as they are about trying to effect that change. To ask what works and what is useful change means asking what our possible actions are and, of course, how things could be different. Ultimately, this can be decided only by the therapeutic dyad, whose desires, longings, passions, dreads, ideas, and, generally, emotional experiences have innumerable sources and origins. Two therapeutic partners, however, do not decide these things in a vacuum, between themselves—though it may feel that way sometimes—but instead are perpetually shaped and informed by the highly complex and larger socio-cultural-historical contexts in which they are perpetually embedded. Thus, therapeutic action and therapeutic change are unique and specific to each dyad (Bacal 2006, Bacal & Carlton 2010, Bacal 2011) and are intensely contextualized phenomena. In addition, questions about action and change inevitably rest on enormous theoretical, ethical, and epistemological concerns, or *attitudes*. For instance, if we speak about changing the psyche, we first must have a perspective on what the psyche is or is not. If we speak about actions, say, verbal interpretation, we must have some ideas about what it means to speak and to proffer a point of view, including the attitudes we have about such a point of view and about how that perspective came about (e.g., this is *my* truth, this is *the* truth, this is my speculation, this is my imagination, this is my spontaneity, this is *our* construction, and so forth). Even more complicating, we cannot exclude trying to think about what goes on within the realm of the implicit, the non-conscious, the prereflective. Some argue that that is where the action, and change, really reside (Stern et al. 1998). Most certainly, that is usually the realm in which our attitudes get conveyed, at least initially. It is our attitudes, ultimately, that are central to understanding therapeutic action and change.

Complexity

Anesthetized by the presumptions of objectivity and the utility of calmness and reason, many of our psychoanalytic forebears could approach theoretical and clinical conundrums with logic and insight, with clarity of thought, and with knowing the problems—and solutions—before they were really investigated. You knew the patient's psyche, or at least how it worked, before you knew the patient.

As soon as a *difficult patient* began placing *unreasonable* demands upon the analyst, for instance, you knew that the patient was in the grips of his instinctual life and was, well, being unreasonable (see Breuer & Freud 1893). Your task was to make him reasonable, effectively, to bring him around to your reality-based perspective and to enjoin him to relinquish his wishes, desires, and longings—what I think of as the pulse and lifeblood of human life. Unreasonableness, or human subjectivity, could be in many instances understood and accounted for and ultimately set aside in favor of clear, objective thinking. Our scientistic zeitgeist rendered known truths and reality static and experimentally replicable; we had a relatively firm ground on which to stand and from which to build more theory and make reasoned clinical decisions. (This perspective can still be found today in many of the cognitive-behavioral and experimental psychology approaches aimed at molding a person's behavior.) However, in alternative circles, the advent of our paradigm shift of the last seventy-five years or so (Kuhn 1962)—essentially from objectivism to perspectivalism—has transformed our "epistemological arrogance … [into] epistemological humility" (Stolorow 2012, p. 1), or what I playfully refer to as *epistemological ineptitude*. This shift repositioned human subjectivity not only as centrally implicated in how we perceive and experience ourselves and the world but also as the principal vehicle of understanding and connecting with others more meaningfully. Interestingly, a close examination of the evolution of the countertransference literature from the early 1900s to the present reflects this shift in our attitude toward human subjectivity, how we think of it, and how we might use it in the service of therapeutic action.[3] In contemporary psychoanalysis and psychotherapy, this attitude is no more powerfully witnessed than in the development of contemporary relational theory; the simultaneous, mutual, and reciprocal influences of multiple subjective beings are the medium of emotional life, of working through problems, and of positive development. As Cooper (2004) remarks, "whether we like it or not, as a human being the analyst will be irrepressibly himself or herself—and why not own up to it and use it to help us understand what goes on in analytic process" (p. 534). Contemporary thinkers now generally embrace what more traditional analysts and therapists might have been squeamish about owning up to as the sine qua non of sound therapeutic work.

One facet of this book concerns the role of explanatory frameworks—our attempts at making sense of things—and the attitudes, frequently implicit and not-so-conscious, that accompany them.[4] In particular, it underscores one specific explanatory framework based on a perspective that quite literally has revolutionized our world and how we think of it today. No one person or group of people invented it (i.e., it is not rooted in any one person's vision or cherished ideas), which is very much to its and our advantage, nor was it originally organized to inform theoretical and clinical psychoanalysis. These are a few of the reasons I have been drawn to it over the last fifteen years. Its language is evocative, albeit cumbersome, though one does not have to speak its language to make use of its concepts. I am speaking of complexity theory and, for the purposes of considering psychoanalysis and psychotherapy, what I refer to as *psychoanalytic complexity*.

The introduction of complexity theory to psychoanalysis and psychoanalytically informed therapies in the last thirty years has been revolutionary, if riddled with personal reactions of perplexity and suspicion; and I do not use the term *revolutionary* lightly. This perspective, of which there are innumerable facets and emphases, has altered profoundly our more traditional presumptions about the individual person, the emergence (and dissociation) of affect and emotional meaning, and the nature of relationships. If there had remained any doubts about the illusion of isolated minds and the internal forces to which they were relentlessly subject, any doubts about the myopia of subjectivist and individualist perspectives, the inculcation of a complexity sensibility into our field has radically overturned them. Clinically, this has been enormously beneficial. The more explicit paradigm shift of the last thirty years, from objectivism to perspectivalism (Mitchell 1988, 1993, 1996, 1997, 2000; Orange 1992, 1993, 2001, 2002, 2003, 2008), from Cartesianism to contextualism (Atwood & Stolorow 1984; Stolorow 2007; Stolorow & Atwood 1979, 1992; Stolorow, Atwood, & Orange 2002; Stolorow, Brandchaft, & Atwood 1987), has been concretized and extended in vital ways by the complexity sensibility with which this book is centrally concerned.

Acknowledging the foundational distinction between lived emotional experience and its concomitant meanings, on the one hand, and the working explanations for the sources of such experience and meanings, on the other hand, is a vital prerequisite for grasping what psychoanalytic complexity offers theorists and clinicians alike. It is essential that we know in what dimension of discourse we are thinking and speaking at a given point in time; are we describing lived emotional experience (the *phenomenological*) or theorizing and otherwise trying to account for such experience through explanation (the *explanatory*)? In the absence of such acknowledging, we remain conceptually muddled and confused. This book aims at ameliorating this confusion.

Moreover, liberating ourselves from the presumption that selfhood and worldhood always operate in (and are explained by) the way they feel to us, and thus ending our centuries-long propensity to reify lived emotional experience, reveals a multitude of dimensions of explanatory discourse, such as the interpenetration of experiential worlds and the inextricability of past, present, and imagined future (Loewald 1972). Theorists and clinicians perpetually struggle with the omnipresent tension between the presumption of interconnectedness between persons relentlessly embedded in socio-cultural-historical contexts, on the one hand, and the assumption that individuals seek and experience personal individuality, agency, autonomy, self-reliance, and authenticity, on the other hand (Frie & Coburn 2011). This struggle has led to the employment of mixed (and sometimes contradictory) models of understanding emotional life, some often grafted onto others. Psychoanalytic complexity obviates the need to invoke contradictory models for explanatory purposes. In this light, theories of the *intrapsychic* or notions of one's *internal world*, for example, become rich sources of phenomenological description but no longer reflect logical explanatory frameworks for accounting for lived emotional experience.

Not all complexity theorists share the same interest in every facet of this paradigm. Each seems to be grabbing a different part of the proverbial complexity elephant. Some underscore the concepts of self-criticality, emergence, and nonlinearity; some the concepts of irreducibility and autocatalysm; whereas others privilege recurrency, novelty, and perturbation (some of the concepts that are highlighted in subsequent chapters). There are many aspects of this perspective, each quite specific, fascinating, and useful in its own right. Overall, though, whatever aspect of the theory one considers, complexity theory historically has been employed primarily as a retrospective tool, one that might explain what has already happened. How did our biological systems organize themselves and create new life? How did astronomical bodies spanning our universe arrange themselves into such specific and intricate patterns? How does emotional life, including the meaning-making process, emerge from the outset of life and throughout the life span; and, of course, in the consultation room between two or more individuals, how does desirable change coalesce? And, as alluded to earlier, what *is* desirable change? Who decides that? We may be able to answer some of these questions in interesting, albeit speculative, ways, retrospectively, but as clinicians who perpetually face the clinical present and the clinical future (and especially as clinicians who are considering more contemporary perspectives in psychoanalysis and psychotherapy), we want to know how to apply new ideas and concepts in useful ways and how to effect positive change. And thus, an additional and primary facet of this book concerns how a contemporary complexity sensibility might be applied or, more accurately, gets applied, through the powerful medium of our largely implicit attitudes—how it might insinuate itself into our clinical work and ultimately inform therapeutic action and positive change. This speaks to the application of a retrospective explanatory framework prospectively to the clinical surround that necessarily will inform how we understand what is unfolding in real time and how we determine our aims and actions—what we might do next. Fundamentally, this book explores a model of psychoanalytic complexity, the clinical attitudes that naturally emanate from it, and how such a theoretical and clinical sensibility changes emotional lives and their corresponding relationships.

Complexity theory—a multidisciplinary and now transdisciplinary explanatory framework employed to understand how systems work—has a rich and varied history embedded in a variety of fields, such as physics, molecular biology, meteorology and, as mentioned previously, the study of slime mold. Now more recently applied to psychological systems and, in particular, to psychoanalysis, complexity theory is expanding our understanding of human complex adaptive systems in exciting and challenging directions. It sheds a much more radical light on the central and relentless role of context in understanding emotional life and the meaning-making process. We have moved from the notion of teaching the patient (Freud 1919), to learning from the patient (Casement 1992; Ferenczi 1928; Kohut 1984), and now to learning from the dynamic, fluid, and unpredictable systems of which each of us is but a component. If we learn nothing else from acknowledging our personal situatedness (Frie 2011) in all these interpenetrating psychological systems, we do grasp that we are fundamentally epistemologically inept beings; we can never grasp a God's-eye view of what gives rise to specific emotional experiences and meanings, always fluid and transforming from one moment to the next, despite our occasional and welcome glimpses of delimited and emergent truth and reality. A psychoanalytic complexity sensibility is indeed humbling and conveys a deeper respect for the complexity of each individual, of each therapeutic dyad, and for the painfully engraved limits of our knowledge.

Attitudes

In thinking about how a psychoanalytic complexity sensibility informs our ideas about therapeutic action, I turn to a familiar, vital, and omnipresent source of information—our attitudes, both implicit and explicit, which inform much of what happens in the therapeutic setting. This is not a new concept by any means; however, I believe it has not received the amount of attention it deserves. While Freud and his followers were extolling and elaborating the necessity for objectivity, clear-mindedness, and the exacting technique of a surgeon in their clinical work—certainly an attitude in its own right!—a much less obvious undercurrent was under way in the early part of the twentieth century: that is, a more explicit consideration of the force of the attitude(s) that each individual brings to bear on the relationship situation. For example, recall Edward Glover's fleeting comment from 1937, embedded in what otherwise was pure Freudian dogma, that "a prerequisite of the efficiency of interpretation is the attitude, the true unconscious attitude of the analyst to his patients" (p. 131). There are many other instances that reflect an explicit appreciation of the powerful role of conscious and non-conscious attitudes in psychoanalysis—certainly, for examples, in the work of Aron (1996), Ferenczi (1928), Friedman (1978, 1988, 2005), Heimann (1950), Hoffman (1994, 2009), Little (1951), Orange (1995, 2011), Sander (1992, 2002), Winnicott (1949), and many others. Here, I define attitudes rather broadly and certainly include a multitude of historical and contemporary notions about transference and countertransference—added to which are concepts such as invariant organizing principles (Stolorow 1995), emotional convictions (Orange 1995), prejudice (Gadamer 1991), philosophical outlook, theoretical background (D. B. Stern 2012), one's past, present, and imagined future (Loewald 1972), situated personal experience (Frie 2011, p. 14), and so forth. The concept of attitude will be examined further in Chapter 2.

This book aims to address, through clinical example, some of the key attitudes, derived from psychoanalytic complexity, that are responsible for therapeutic action in psychoanalysis and psychotherapy. Some of these complexity attitudes are found in other psychoanalytic paradigms as well, such as intersubjective systems theory (Bonn 2010; Sperry 2011; Stolorow, Atwood & Orange 1998, 2002; Sucharov 1994, 2002; Trop, Burke & Trop 2002); self- and motivational systems theory (Lichtenberg, Lachmann & Fosshage 1992, 1996, 2011); developmental systems self psychology (Shane 2006; Shane, Shane & Gales 1997); specificity theory (Bacal 2006, Bacal & Carlton 2010, Bacal 2011); and relational theory (Ghent 2002; Harris 2005; Mitchell 2000; Pickles 2006; Piers 2005; Seligman 2005; Thelen 2005; VanDerHeide 2011; Weisel-Barth 2006), lending support to the crucial and essential role attitudes play in the healing relationship.

For instance, one complexity attitude pertains to how we hold in our minds the notion of *the self*. Like it or not, each of us is relentlessly and inextricably ensconced in elaborate human and non-human complex systems from which there is only one escape. We tend not to think of ourselves in this way, not to experience ourselves as such. Even to speak this way, to speak of selves, suggests that we *have* selves. Sometimes, we speak of them almost as appendages in relative states of repair or disrepair, cohesion or fragmentation (Kohut 1984). Experientially speaking—meaning, if we are considering things entirely on the basis of personal, felt, lived experience—we may or may not have a self at all (Atwood, Orange & Stolorow 2002), though generally, ecstatic and mystical experiences aside, we much prefer having one—a self ideally characterized by creativity, autonomy, agency, authorship, ownership, love, and safety— than not. Explanatorily speaking—meaning, if we are considering things on the basis of trying to explain experience, to account for the phenomenological through theoretical constructs—the self (as in independent, individual, isolated, unattached entity) is an illusion, albeit a very real one, an illusion that is actually "distributively structured among multiple islands of relational experience" (Pizer 1996, p. 503).[5] Each of us is the product and property of larger, highly interactive, interconnected complex systems.

Here is one among many ways in which to imagine the self. Drawing from the work of Taylor (2001), think of yourself for a moment as two types of screens (admittedly not a particularly pleasant thought): first, the type of screen onto which material of all kinds (visual, biological, physical, emotional, spiritual) is projected, and think of the projector as the larger array of interpenetrating, nonlinear, complex systems that exist everywhere; and then the second type of screen, a semipermeable membrane that filters material, like the screen on a patio door. Essentially, think of your self as simultaneously both a projection and a filter, just as a photon, by analogy, is simultaneously a particle and a wave. In this way, we are at once a nodal point for the emergence and expression of larger complex (relational) systems *and* a unique determiner of what, exactly and specifically, emerges from and gets expressed about those systems. This is not to suggest by any means that you, or what you think of as your self, are not real. Quite the contrary! One's experiential world is more real than anything I can think of. It is the currency of our lives and of living lives that are so embedded and intertwined in what we think of as the world. As Orange (2001) reminds us, we inhabit the world just as the world inhabits us. It is just that our experiential worlds are not exactly *ours*—they just frequently feel like ours. And there are many more attitudes to consider as well—a principal topic of this book.

How might this sensibility, this attitude, inform what we do clinically—inform how we think implicitly, how we behave, what clinical choices we make, essentially, how we *are*? How might we gain new attitudes and use them? Certainly not by trying to apply a new theory with its invariable attendant prescriptions. Any attitude that is discovered and that is presumably useful generally does not just get applied. Rather, studying ideas and thinking about their possible corresponding attitudes and implications, truly considering them and then setting them aside, radically transforms the trajectory of the therapeutic relationship. Once studied, tried on for size, reflected upon, and then placed aside, new ideas, if they are worth anything, will have already altered something of your emotional world and your clinical sensibility. As Friedman (2005) notes, "theories set the therapist's attitude, the attitude affects the background forces, and the total effect of all of that constitutes the significance of the theories for psychoanalytic treatment" (p. 418). And I would add, the therapist's attitude informs her theories (Stolorow & Atwood 1979), and the background forces affect her attitudes as well. Friedman also astutely acknowledges that

> [a]nalysts had not realized that even the most specific comment expresses a rather broad attitude toward a patient. A comment is received by patients not as a biopsy of their mind, but as a way of being looked at by someone who prefers, for some reason, to see them that way. It is recognized as an effort to persuade them [though, I would add, not necessarily always] to take some attitude, or move in a certain direction, or respond to the analyst in some way or other (Raphling, 1996, 2002; Shapiro, 2002)…[T]he patient cannot pick up just [a] fact without the perspective from which it is seen (or thought to be seen), and the personal attitude that would be associated with such a perspective.
>
> (Friedman 2005, p. 422).

Just as context is everything, so is attitude. And thus, technically, it is not something we do per se but, rather, it is something that we perhaps will simply *find ourselves doing*.

Thus, to extend our use of complexity theory into realms other than solely grasping an explanatory framework, it behooves us to explore the implicit and explicit attitudes that emanate from adopting such a psychoanalytic complexity perspective and how these attitudes impact the change process. The following attitudes—by no means an exhaustive list—are addressed and elaborated in the following chapters and infiltrate the spirit of the clinical narratives.

1 *An unrelenting respect for the complexity of human experiencing and personal individuality*: Emotional experience and its corresponding meanings can no longer be understood as solely the result of neuronal firing encased in a hardened shell or simply the unfolding of a preexisting or predesigned genetic pattern. In a world of complex systems, no one set of

components of a system or what we might think of as predesign can be held responsible for what emerges next. Being quintessentially contextualized beings, relentlessly shaping and being shaped by a highly specific and dynamic world, we humans are profoundly irreducible and are perpetually in transition from one state to the next. We certainly cannot be reduced to a diagnostic category if we are to maintain our sense of uniqueness, individuality, and passion for the unexpected.

2 *Our relentless embeddedness in contexts from which we can never extricate ourselves*: A spirit of unremitting contextualism, found in several paradigms such as intersubjective systems theory (Stolorow 1997), is foundational to a psychoanalytic complexity sensibility.

3 *Being continually informed by our history, our current state, and our environment, and the lines between these sources of our experience remaining forever indeterminate*: This assumption is essential in understanding the emergence of emotional life and the meanings we attribute to it. An aspect of our existence as quintessentially contextualized beings is that we have a history that impels and propels us, we have a present in which our lives unfold in our perpetually moving toward what will be our next present, and we have an environment that we act upon just as it acts upon us (see Heidegger's concept of *ecstatic temporality*, 1927). Here, environment can be defined in any way you wish—it is up to you. It is anything that you consider outside of or other than what you consider to be your self from one moment to the next and, of course, whatever that may be will change and fluctuate as time passes. What is clinically crucial is that this attitude assumes that we can never relegate a facet of a person's experiential world (e.g., an emotional conviction or an affect state) solely to his history, to his current state of mind, or to his environment. The exact line between these three sources of emotional life is forever indeterminate.

4 *Autocatalysm and recurrence*: This attitude, that the very components of a system produce their own agent of change and that what emerges from within a given system can feed back upon itself, altering its previous state, profoundly alters how we traditionally had conceptualized therapeutic action; that is, the notion that one person acting on or toward another is what effects change. In this more contemporary light, it allows for the likelihood that the agent of change emerges as a product and property of the relational system itself.

5 *Emergence, nonlinearity, and valuing the "feeling" of complexity, in the phenomenological sense*: This refers to the process of bringing emotional themes and relating to life and to learning to sense and recognize its emergence. In complexity theory, the word *complexity* has very specific and sometimes discrepant meanings (e.g., the state of an open system and the characteristic of its not being reducible or compressible to something smaller or simpler), which are discussed in detail in Chapter 4. And normally it is not used to describe an experience (the *phenomenological*). Instead,

it describes a particular state (the realm of the *explanatory*) of a system, one poised for imminent change. This renders an attitude that invites the therapeutic dyad to sense and feel when their system is in flux and ready to change in—ideally—positive directions. These moments can be marked, addressed, and commented upon. A dyad can learn to sense when their system is in flux and headed in unpredictable directions, which is good, as opposed to living in the quagmire of what feels like the repetitive, the usual, the familiar, and the comfortable. This attitude also refers to the nonlinearity of complex human systems: that seemingly small events may lead to large and meaningful outcomes.

6 *Embracing epistemological ineptitude*: As alluded to previously, this attitude conveys a deep respect for the limits of our knowledge and aims to keep us alert to experiences of resolution, equilibrium, complacency, and generally settling into the false presumption that we have things pretty much figured out and do not have much more to learn (see Orange 2003a, and *perspectival realism* and *fallibilism*).

7 *Distinctions between dimensions of discourse—the phenomenological and the explanatory/metaphysical*: This attitude underscores the importance of not conflating two very distinct levels of discourse—one pertaining to lived, subjective experience and the other to the explanatory frameworks we might invoke to understand and describe such experience. One result of conflating the two is the reification of dimensions of experience, essentially reducing them down to constructs that then take on a concrete life of their own.

8 *Conundrum of personal situatedness, emotional responsibility, and potential (finite) freedom*: This attitude encourages us to consider that we humans are *thrown* (Heidegger 1927) into life circumstances that are largely not of our making, that we often simply *discover* ourselves in emotional and relational circumstances, sometimes painfully so, that leave us with that sense of *how did I get here?*—*that* feeling of, to paraphrase the Talking Heads (1980), this is not my beautiful life, this is not what I designed or intended for myself! How *did* I get here? It also encourages us then to consider assuming responsibility for where indeed we *do* find ourselves and to accept, without sliding into defeat and a malignant sense of fatedness (Strenger 1998), our current situatedness—to really *own* it. And finally, this attitude then invites us to consider what potential, though finite, freedom we might garner from our current life situation. What might we make of ourselves, now, moving forward in time? What might we make of ourselves, given what we have been handed and given that we are quintessentially creative beings with the capacity to reflect and imagine? This is an attitude of appreciating a sense of constraint in concert with the potential for future self-authorship and self-ownership.

9 *Radical hope*: Phrased in the spirit of the work of Jonathan Lear (2007), this attitude essentially speaks to the experience of having some hope for a better, imagined future, despite the fact that we may not be able to envision

specifically in what form that future might coalesce. It is an attitude that considers what courage there might be to envision something different and positive, despite our inability to picture it clearly in the current moment. This type of hope may be realized given our understanding that complex systems are not rule-driven or predetermined but are quite literally open to change in ways that we may not yet be able to imagine.

10 *Spirit of inquiry* (Kohut, 1984; Lichtenberg et al. 1992; Mitchell 2000; Stolorow & Atwood 1992)/*hermeneutics of trust* (Orange 2011): This attitude, certainly not originating from complexity theory, is nevertheless quintessentially representative of complexity and thus deserving of emphasis. That is because a complexity sensibility argues that when change is about to occur, we can never really know how that change will appear and/or whether it will be useful change at that. Keeping an open attitude of curiosity and thus inquiry (not to be confused with grilling your patient with questions!) encourages anticipating surprise and appreciating novelty—that sense conveyed to others that we can never know what will emerge next, nor can we ever know, before we get there, what emotional experiences and their corresponding meanings may be in store for us. Orange's (2011) *hermeneutics of trust* resonates well with a true spirit of inquiry, in that it conveys to the patient that we are here to discover, together, the emergence of unique emotional life and to be open to surprise, as opposed to assuming we know, more or less, what already resides in the experiential world of the patient and that the patient is usually intent on deceiving us.

I invite you to keep these attitudes in mind as you delve into the following pages, which aim to address how a complexity sensibility, inadvertently emergent over the last 100 years or so, might inform alternative ways of thinking and working clinically. The initial portion of this book (Chapters 1, 2, and 3) addresses, with the help of clinical material, the background of thinking about therapeutic action and change and the inescapable role of attitudes. It then proceeds to explore some of the essential ideas embedded in complexity theory and how they might be applied—or how they *get* applied—to the clinical setting (Chapters 4 and 5). Chapter 5 is primarily clinical in nature and reflects how these attitudes inform the trajectory of the clinical relationship and the emergence of the change process.

Notes

1 From Jack Drescher's interview with Stephen Mitchell, 1994 in *The White Society Voice*, New York: William Alanson White Institute and the William Alanson White Psychoanalytic Society, p. 3. Reprinted with permission, ©1994, The William Alanson White Psychoanalytic Society and ©2013, Contemporary Psychoanalysis (Journal of the William Alanson White Institute and the William Alanson White Psychoanalytic Society), All Rights Reserved.

2 Lawrence Friedman, (2005) 'Psychoanalytic treatment: thick soup or thin gruel?' *Psychoanalytic Inquiry* 25, 4: 418–439. Reprinted by permission of Taylor & Francis (http://www.tandfonline.com

3 For a stimulating review of the countertransference literature, see: Abend 1989; Arnetoli 1999; Aron 1996; Bacal & Thomson 1996; Balint & Balint 1939; Bernstein 1999; Cooper 1996; Epstein & Feiner 1979; Freud 1910a, 1912, 1913b, 1914; Frie 1997; Gill 1983; Orr 1954; Racker 1968; Reik 1948; Sands 1997; Searles 1979; Stern 1997; Stolorow, Orange, & Atwood 1998; Tower 1956.

4 See Greenberg (1981) for a thorough discussion of the relationship between description and prescription in psychoanalytic theory.

5 This was the organizing theme for a recent International Association for Psychoanalytic Self Psychology Annual Conference titled "Is Self An Illusion?" October, 2012, Washington, DC.

Chapter 1

Complexity, Therapeutic Action, and Jack

You boys going to get somewhere, or just going?

—Jack Kerouac[1]

Therapeutic Action

Therapeutic action, as a concept, process, and preoccupation, has a rich and varied history, one primarily concerned with reducing emotional suffering. Arguably dating from Breuer and Freud (1893)—not that philosophy, science, and religion previously had not been concerned with curing disturbances of the soul—notions of psychopathology (what presumably causes suffering) and treatment (what presumably reduces or cures it) were inevitably informed by our then-current and inescapable worldviews about truth, reality, and knowledge (epistemology); the good (ethics); and the beautiful (aesthetics). From these worldviews emanated presumptions about the substance and machinations of the psyche. They were also shaped by our needs, wishes, desires, and longings. None of us exists without being situated somewhere, ensconced in a perspective or *prejudice* (Gadamer 1991) from which we perceive and experience the world and ourselves (Stolorow et al. 2002) and from which there is only one exit. There is no view from nowhere (Nagel 1986). How we come to define suffering and dysfunction is largely based on the sociocultural and hence personal situatedness of the individual, or groups of individuals (Frie 2010). Through the lens of a worldview that pathologizes painful affect (something to be excised) while privileging dispassionate logic and clarity of intellect, for example, aspects of one's emotional life become the repudiated and the enemy, and rationality, depending on how it is defined, becomes our weapon (A. Freud 1976). This view was especially pernicious in light of the fact that, prior to our paradigm shift of the last fifty years or so, it frequently was a person of authority (e.g., the doctor, the therapist) who decided what was to be excised and what was *rational*.

Thus, ideas about therapeutic action necessarily rest on presumptions and conclusions we have about how the world works, about what is wrong and what needs changing, about what we want, and about what it means, for us human individuals, to suffer. Alternatively stated, our attitudes about these fundamental questions (for which traditionally we have often felt we have answers) inform a multitude of conclusions about psychopathology, development, cure, transference, defenses, our clinical decision-making process, and the trajectory of our clinical relationships in performing psychoanalysis and psychotherapy. This chapter has as its point of departure the main historical themes around which therapeutic action and change have revolved over time; its principal focus is my experience with my patient, Jack.

In considering therapeutic action, it is important to distinguish between the action of change (what is done to effect change, for example, a verbal interpretation) and what gets changed (for instance, the structure of one's psyche or the character of one's experiential world or one's relational patterns). For Sigmund Freud and many of his followers, the structure of the psyche (id, ego, superego) and the dynamics of the psyche (the relationship between the structural parts, including the management of unconscious, preconscious, and conscious material) were what got changed, whereas the action of change presumably resided in the conveyance of insight and knowledge via verbal interpretation by the analyst. The analyst essentially taught the patient what the patient did not know, frequently did not want to know, and perhaps could not know (S. Freud 1919). Repression was lifted, memories were recalled, and instinctual wishes were relinquished and sublimated in the service of health, maturity, and the greater good.

When we think about change, we necessarily ask, Why *don't* people change? Or, alternatively, when they do, why so seemingly slowly? I believe real and reliable change is hard-won because however painful one's organizing principles or emotional themes might be, without them, suddenly stripped of them, one would be plunged into an unmanageable abyss, what Stolorow, Atwood, and Orange (2010) refer to as structureless chaos, or what Bernstein (1983) refers to as Cartesian anxiety. There would be no firm ground left on which to stand. Much better to be organized and oriented to the world through suffering and perhaps traumatic repetition than to free oneself from those shackles and risk losing the essential ground on which one has stood and from which one has derived a sense of felt reality and clarity, a *sense of the real* (Coburn 2001a). Eric Erikson once said that "a negative identity is better than no identity" (R. D. Stolorow, personal communication, December 16, 2010). There are other reasons we rely on whatever organizing principles we may have and with which we may be suffering. Maintaining ties to vital attachment figures (Ainsworth & Bell 1974; Bowlby 1969, 1973, 1980; Brandchaft 2007; Brandchaft, Doctors & Sorter 2010; Main 1993), for instance, is a compelling one. Generally, we are drawn to the familiar and the safe, like the proverbial moth to the flame. Let us turn to my patient Jack and me for a moment, as we begin to think about complexity, therapeutic action, and change.

Complexity and Jack

The work of complexity is perhaps no more profoundly evident than in witnessing the unexpected, abrupt, sometimes startling shifts in human experiencing and relating that flow from the psychoanalytic relationship. This was certainly the case with Jack, who struggled with an excruciatingly impoverished self-esteem and a propensity for social withdrawal and isolation. Distracted and preoccupied, his mother had left him in his stroller in a supermarket when he was quite young, and it was not until she had stowed her groceries, closed the trunk of her minivan, and chatted with a friend that she realized her negligence and retrieved him from the store manager; this was his model scene (Lichtenberg 2008). He was either forgettable or grotesque. Two-and-a-half years into a three-times-per-week analytic therapy, something hit both of us like a lightning bolt, though I think I was more startled than he was. Jack, then forty-five years of age and divorced for a little longer than I had known him, had been contemplating internet dating and the likelihood of a future relationship (or the lack thereof). As much as he yearned for closeness and intimacy, he knew that his potential female companion would discover fairly quickly upon meeting him, or seeing a picture of him, his true beast-like nature. He would refer to himself as a creature somehow akin to Frankenstein's monster. These references conjured for me the sense of loneliness, isolation, rage, self-hatred, and longing of the monster that Mary Shelley so beautifully portrayed in her novel, and Jack would occasionally perk up from his otherwise rather depressed and subdued affect—an ambiance that often left us both feeling doomed—when I made explicit these associations. Yes, he would say, that's just how a woman would experience me if I showed her what I look like. Despite my intermittent interpretations that perhaps there was something of how he felt about himself (monster-like, unapproachable, repellant) that had infiltrated and colored how he experienced his physical appearance, he remained irrevocably ensconced in this conviction. Through his eyes, he actually looked like a monster of sorts, not so hideous that people would shriek and run away but awful enough that he would remain either disgusting and unwanted or, at best, quite forgettable in the eyes and minds of others. Rarely would he look in the mirror. Photos generally had been out of the question.

These dimensions of his self-experience intensified when he finally dared to have his picture taken by a colleague who said he knew something about photography. He had reached an impasse at the internet dating threshold when he discovered that he needed to post a photograph—something he was loathe to do, given his perception of his beast-like nature. He was tormented as he anxiously awaited his colleague's digital photos of him. Not surprisingly, Jack hated the photos immediately, and I silently assumed that that was the end of his dating attempts. There is nothing quite like having a painful emotional conviction confirmed. What emerged, though, much to the surprise of both of us, was his exclamation that he thought he could have taken much better photos and that, in fact, he had rushed to purchase his own camera, take his own photographs of himself, and promptly posted them on his internet dating web site, all within the span of a day! He was quite proud not only of his accomplishment but also of how he appeared in the photos. Where was the monster I had been treating for two-and-a-half years?

There are many ways of speculating about and understanding what had emerged here, but doubtless both Jack and his sometimes pessimistic and frustrated analyst had undergone a transformation in their combined experiential worlds. This was the therapeutic equivalent of the Belousov-Zhabotinsky reaction in chemistry— the sudden and unexpected emergence of strikingly discernible patterns and colors in an otherwise clear, stable, and predictable chemical solution—in which the appearance of predictability and linearity collapses, revealing the actual fluidity and unpredictability of a system. This dovetails with our fifth attitude, that of "emergence, nonlinearity, and valuing the *feeling* of complexity, in the phenomenological sense." It was also a striking illustration of the autocatalytic behavior of a complex adaptive system (our fourth attitude, that of "autocatalysm and recurrence"), in that the relational system itself, composed of Jack, myself, and a variety of other essential people in his life (past, present, and imagined future), self-organized in a manner that produced its own agent of change. In that sense, it would be impossible to claim what or who, exactly, that agent is, given the multitude of variables at play. In molecular biology, we might be able to identify, in retrospect, the specific catalyst implicated in the transformation of new cell structure, but the catalyst is not so easily identifiable when considering the medium of emotional experience.

An especially illuminating instance of this phenomenon occurred much earlier in Jack's treatment. Heretofore I had experienced him as affectively constricted, highly measured, and self-consciously methodical in his choice of words; he was playing to an audience about to castigate him for the slightest sign of emotional life or creativity. He was organized and had a complete, pre-designed card catalogue of responses to any questions aimed at encouraging reflection or experimentation. I was the unforgiving job interviewer for whom he had better supply the right answers, lest I forget him or find him monstrous. The vaguer my inquiry, the more anxious he got.

During one exchange that was particularly anxiety-provoking for both of us, in which he was speaking about his having little sense of space in his life in which to be creative vis-à-vis his interest in painting and building things, I asked him whether he had ideas about how he had come to feel so constricted and prohibited. As he reached for one of his standard-issue, card catalogue responses, I noticed he hesitated, his eyes momentarily glancing at the floor, as if he were stumped in an otherwise fast-paced game of Jeopardy with millions at stake. Despite the anxiety, however, I ever-so-briefly noticed a gentle, soft, and enlivened expression wash over his face. I felt I had been given a nanosecond glimpse into an alive, accessible, and creative Jack: the Jack, it seemed, I had been waiting for, though I previously hadn't realized I had been waiting for anyone or anything at all. As he quickly recovered from his shameful stumble, not having located the particular card he was searching for but having found another, I quickly interrupted him and asked whether he had just noticed something. He said, "No, not really; what do you mean?" I shared with him my experience, describing my perception of him as particularly accessible, alive, unsure, and perplexed in that all-too-brief moment. He smiled with recognition, saying that that was exactly how he never allowed himself to be. He then began to hyperventilate and sob, rather violently actually, occasionally glancing at me through his tears. As he made to bolt from his chair, apparently preparing for a lightening-speed exit, I said that perhaps it might be worth our while for him to consider staying. As he sat back down, I said that I thought we had hit upon something quite meaningful, something that perhaps we were both after, and maybe we could speak about it. He seemed moved by this, his eyes widening. What followed was an intense and elaborate exchange about the terror and shame he felt at the emergence of such a sudden reaction—one that he couldn't possibly understand; there was no card in his catalogue for this, and it terrified him. I told him that I thought I may have acknowledged something special about him—a moment of Jack with no prefabricated responses, no filter to stave off my inevitable attack or abandonment, a moment of real life and emotional presence—and that this perhaps was quite moving for him and subsequently quite alarming as well. He agreed. I believe this incident was pivotal in sending our relationship off into new directions, generating a trajectory shift in our system in which we were now co-adapting to each other in different ways (our fifth attitude). This shift was punctuated by, or perhaps reflected in, our final exchange as he walked out the door: Jack said, "Gosh, I'm sorry about all that—I feel like I should apologize"—to which I quipped, "That's all right; I'll let it go, but just this once." When he smirked at me, I again witnessed a sense of surprise and aliveness wash across his face. In the brief span of that momentary exchange, we witnessed the rapidly alternating and competing attractor states[2] that increasingly emerged over the course of treatment and that came to characterize our relationship. Obviously, humor and irony, always emergent properties and products of relational systems, played an important role here as well (Lear 2007).

A complexity perspective might suggest that I had provided a perturbation, with its predictable ensuing anxiety (Trop, Burke, & Trop 2002), to an otherwise repetitive system, momentarily transforming it into a transformative system (Lachmann 2000). However, it is important to underscore that we cannot claim to know, exactly, what the perturbation was. Who, really, is perturbing whom in the psychotherapeutic system? In truth, the perturbation here was an emergent property of the system, as I believe it always is, not something I did *to* Jack that can account for the therapeutic effects of this encounter. Jack was perturbing the system as much as I was, via his brief, unexpected, and enlivening "stumble." His brief and sudden doorknob slide into shame and apology was as perturbing to me and to our system as my rejoinder to him was to him and to our system.

These are instances of using psychoanalytic complexity to understand and describe more richly and usefully the appearance of change, its sense of emergence and unpredictability, the system's autocatalytic tendencies, the benefit of living near *the tipping point*, and the acknowledgement that the responsibility for emotional experience and emotional meaning are distributed throughout the system's constituents. However, in what manner can we say that the theory gets applied in clinical work? As argued throughout this book, a revealing entry point into answering this question lies in considering the essential attitudes derived from a complexity sensibility.

First, a psychoanalytic complexity perspective doubtless embraces the relatively tried and true assumptions about therapeutic action in psychoanalysis. This would include the investigation, understanding, and articulation of the patient's intersubjectively derived organizing themes and affect that contour the patient's experiential world (Stolorow et al. 2002); the patient and analyst's self/ other configurations that are brought to light, engaged, and experientially lived out in the context of the therapeutic relationship (Davies 2004; Mitchell 2000); the patient's selfobject needs and the inevitable disruption and repair cycles that permeate the therapeutic relationship (Kohut 1984); an appreciation for the specificity of fit between analyst and patient (Bacal 2011); and the patient/ analyst's implicit (non-symbolized and non-verbal symbolized) relating that may or may not come to light but that often determines the ultimate trajectory of their combined experiential worlds (Boston Change Process Study Group 2007; Fosshage 2005). In other words, grasp any part of the elephant you want (but watch out for his feet). Second, however, the mutative effects of a psychoanalytic complexity perspective largely rest in the fundamental attitudes they imbue in the therapeutic relationship and in the attitudes at which the therapeutic dyad ultimately arrives.

From one standpoint, we could entertain a simple disconfirmation theory (for instance, via passing transference tests [Weiss 1986]), that what *transformed* Jack generally was my disconfirming his relational expectancies, indeed my not finding in Jack—and my not responding to Jack in the manner of—the shame-ridden, forgettable monster he felt himself to be. Or, alternatively, we could consider an integration theory, that what was mutative for Jack was our combined willingness to bring to life, in the context of our relationship, a host of previously sequestered and/or dissociated self-other configurations, on both our parts (Davies 2004). We could also invoke insight theory alone, adopting the perspective that our investigation and understanding of the origins of his experience led him to grasp how he came to experience himself and the world in the way that he did, and then all was good—the demands of instinctual life relinquished or reorganized (S. Freud 1933). Moreover, we could argue a deficit theory, that Jack's deficits in his self-structure were essentially repaired, or filled in, as a result of an attuned selfobject presence capable of withstanding the inevitable negative reactions to disillusionment and disruption in the course of treatment (Kohut 1984).

Instead, I believe what proved most useful, at least in this particular treatment situation, were the systemically derived attitudes about emotional experience and emotional meaning at which Jack and I arrived during the course of our relationship. Over time, we began to be able to identify what it was like to live in a system that was either too ordered or too random. We learned, through investigation and experimentation, that Jack's emotional experience was an emergent property of our combined histories, our combined current emotional states, and our combined relational environments—that it was dynamic and did not emanate from an isolated, subjective mental apparatus (or simply from being forgotten in a supermarket).

Fundamentally, I think psychoanalytic complexity is useful in how it alters our essential assumptions about and attitudes toward people, which, in turn, transform how we interact with and relate to others (namely, our patients). It conveys a human sensibility that says, essentially, you are not responsible for your emotional experience, even though ultimately you might want to take responsibility—and at times, *must* take responsibility—for it (our eighth attitude, the "conundrum of personal situatedness, emotional responsibility, and potential [finite] freedom"). It says, you did not create yourself, though you may wish to have—and *can* have—a say in what you think, feel, and do next. It proclaims that your emotional development continues on a nonlinear path, such that who or how you will become is unpredictable, potentially fluid, and emergent as a function of numerous other components of a larger co-adaptive, complex system (our fourth and fifth attitudes). It also says, you are not a category into which you may be assigned for defining, labeling, treating, and conforming (our first attitude—an "unrelenting respect for the complexity of human experiencing and personal individuality"). And it asserts that people can change, and we can never really know a priori what might bring about that change, or whether change ultimately will ever take place (our sixth and ninth attitudes—"embracing epistemological ineptitude" and "radical hope," respectively [Lear 2007]).

More broadly, therapeutic action can be conceptualized as the process of investigating and understanding the experiential world of the patient, especially the specific felt sources and origins of that world. As we know, this necessitates the similar investigation and understanding of the analyst's experiential world as well, including the measured articulation of aspects of it in the context of the therapeutic dialogue. It also includes an ongoing appreciation for (and hopefully, articulation of) the implicit, non-symbolized dimension of experiencing and relational learning (Fosshage 2005) that so powerfully and involuntarily contributes to the co-adaptive, mutually organizing aspects of the relational world the two individuals co-constitute together. (By now, it must be evident that to investigate the experiential world of the patient means also to explore and attempt to account for the greater context of which each of us is an integral constituent.) This process also requires a continual sensitivity to and articulation of what is felt to be most affectively enlivening, self-expansive, self-integrative, and deepening of interpersonal contact. This is not news from the standpoint of a variety of contemporary psychoanalytic paradigms. However, more specifically, it is the expansion of the dyad's collaboratively arrived-at and felt awareness of these sources and origins—past, present, and imagined future—that plays an essential role in the perturbation of the relational system such that the stage is set for the emergence of new, more useful patterns of experience. Importantly, these more useful patterns of experience should not be construed to mean more reality-based, more objective, or truer. Ultimately, these newer experiential contours are sustainable because they are reiterated over time and supported by and throughout the interpenetrating relational systems in the patient's life.

What might this expansion, so central to therapeutic action, look like? And why is this expansion so pivotal to change? Let's return to Jack for a moment. For years, Jack's (and my) interest rested in not just how he experienced himself (heretofore forgettable and monstrous), his history (heretofore awful), and his environment (heretofore sometimes benign, sometimes dangerous) but in *why* he experienced these aspects of his life in these ways. For a long period, Jack was confirmed in the view that the emotional absence of his parents could account for these experiences. He pictured himself as unable to extricate himself from his historical milieu in which his sense of self remained shackled to being forgettable and monstrous and in which his sense of the world remained obstinately critical and abandoning. As we explored these particular dimensions of his experience in the context of our relationship (in which these self-other configurations had intermittently come to life), what became increasingly evident to both of us was not just that our relationship was an evocation of and conduit for his relational history, effectively allowing "old ghosts [to] reawaken to life," "to taste blood," and to be "let loose" (Loewald 1960, p. 29) but that we were both constituting his experiences, in real time and over time, such that we remained as integral a part of what was responsible for his experiential world as was his relational history and his sense of his relational future.

The therapeutic relationship is not solely a means of *working something through* or *resolving conflict* but can more profitably be understood as being an essential source of expansion of an individual's experiential world, in concert with one's history, one's current state of mind, and one's environment, variously defined. Therapeutically, we wish not to arrive and remain at conclusions about our emotional life together that are devoid of this sense of the ongoing complexity of its origins and sources that have been stripped of its sense of context, past, present, and imagined future but rather to expand our awareness of the ongoing, continually shifting, multiple sources that contribute to such experience.

Alternatively stated, if sustainable change in perceptions, meanings, and ways of relating is more likely to occur within a complex adaptive system that is situated more or less between order and chaos, or "poised at the edge of chaos," it is desirable for both patient and analyst to be able to sense and acknowledge when their relationship is headed or is situated in that direction (i.e., away from too much order or too much randomness). This is accomplished through dialogue, yes, but also via the essential spirit that underlies the psychoanalytic relationship: the wish to be curious, to inquire, and to understand (our tenth attitude—a "spirit of inquiry" [Lichtenberg, Lachmann, & Fosshage 2002]).

It is not solely the therapist's willingness and capacity to tolerate the expectable painful affect—the inevitable doom and darkness that sometimes permeates our therapeutic work—that is mutative but the therapist's implicitly conveyed sense that there is more to the patient, and to us, than what we know thus far—that there is more to us than our history, our enactments, and our current, arrived-at conclusions.

Therapeutic Action: Reflections

In thinking about therapeutic action, I wish to revisit for a moment the distinction between *therapeutic action* and *therapeutic change*. For me, therapeutic action denotes those actions authored by and occurring between the patient and the therapist that lead to positive developmental change, whereas therapeutic change refers to the results (of therapeutic action) that are considered by patient and therapist to be useful in advancing the patient's experiential world in a positive direction. Note the absence of specificity in the terms *useful* and *positive*. Therapeutic change is a phenomenon that can be described only a posteriori on an individual basis, not prescriptively beforehand. I believe this is the thrust and beauty of Bacal's theory of specificity (2006, 2011).

The problem of a lack of distinction between therapeutic action and therapeutic change is found in Friedman's (1988) excellent explication of therapeutic action in psychotherapy and psychoanalysis.[3] He draws from psychoanalytic history three essential modes of therapeutic action: insight, attachment (or new relational experience), and psychological integration. The first two, in my view, are examples of therapeutic action, and the third, of therapeutic change. Elsewhere I have argued for the coalescence of the *sense of the real* as a vital element involved in therapeutic action (Coburn 2001a). This is an instance of a combination of the meaning of the terms *action* and *change*, in that the coalescence of the *sense of the real* represents both a transformative element (action) and the result of such a transformation (change). The same dual significance might be found in Aron's (2000) concept of the capacity for self-reflexivity.

In this light, what can complexity theory teach us about therapeutic action and therapeutic change? Do we, for instance, conceptualize therapeutic action as a process whereby new systemic patterns of experience in one context *generalize* to other contexts *outside* of the therapeutic context? If so, how is that supposed to work? Is it ever possible to step *outside* of any context once one has stepped into it? Do we, as subjective beings with multiple relationships, move from one context to (or into) another, with similar systemic contours of experience being activated along the way? In other words, do we *carry* our organizing principles or contours of experience around with us, as in the Cartesian sense of carrying around an intrapsychic life, fantasies (or phantasies) and all? Do we *carry* relational expectancies (Beebe & Lachmann 1998) or self and object representations around with us, or are there alternative ways of understanding the appearance of similarly thematized patterns of experience in evidence across multiple contexts (a phenomenon that traditionally has been considered a form of transference)?

Furthermore, if the organizing principles or contours of experience that are being investigated in the analytic milieu are necessarily *systemic* organizing principles, co-constituted from within the analytic dyad, how can we ever reach the principles that are particularly germane to the patient's history and historical context? And furthermore, do we need to? Theoretically speaking, what is the difference between those patterns of experience that are said to be systemically derived in the context of psychoanalysis and psychotherapy, truly unique properties and components of the analytic dyad, and those that are felt to be more central to the patient's family of origin, more germane to the unique patterns of experience originating from the patient's history? Or is this a false distinction? Who, or what, exactly, is being investigated anyway?

This latter question has been explored and elaborated by theorists such as Aron (1996), Mitchell (1993), and Stolorow, Atwood, and Orange (2002). They underscore that the subject matter of psychoanalysis is necessarily not just the subjectivity of the patient but that of the analyst as well. This has been referred to in other contexts as examining transference-countertransference configurations in the analytic dyad. However, a more radical contextualist approach does not just recognize the necessity of including the subjectivity of the analyst in the exploration process but instead chooses to understand all psychological phenomena as components and products of the interface between the two participants, in concert with many other interpenetrating, complex systems, perhaps too numerous to envision. Through the process of *framing* (a concept to be discussed in Chapter 4), systems can be arbitrarily delimited, and some systems can be privileged over others. The spirit of complexity theory, as stated previously, asserts that all psychological phenomena are always the product of the system's history, its current state, and its current environment, and the lines drawn between these three sources of emotional experience cannot be anything but indeterminate.

In light of this more radical contextualism, we are able to account more reasonably for the fact that therapeutic changes said to occur *inside* the consultation room appear to be generalized to relationships forged in the *outside world*. The idea of generalizability—originally a behaviorist concept—heretofore cemented psychoanalytic theorists to the notion of an isolated mind undergoing therapeutic change in response to the interventions of another isolated mind. Those changes, sequestered from and perhaps impervious to the *outside world*, were then thought to be carried around by that individual, just as he or she was thought now to be the proud, post-analysis owner of a transference-free, isolated, intrapsychic world. Being relatively *transference-free*, the patient would be able to experience a wholly objective world, unencumbered by a highly subjective, and distorting, perceiving lens. This traditional view collapses under the weight of our current knowledge of complexity and nonlinear systems.

If we accept that the subject matter of investigation is the perceived patterns of experience coalescing systemically in the consultation room, that they are the result of the self-organization of that system's myriad components, and that these patterns of experiencing evolve and transform largely due to their illumination, how can we then conceptualize the appearance of change in one individual? In the spirit of this theoretical framework, we technically can no longer speak in terms of individual change but rather as systemic change within one system that then has profound repercussions throughout other systems of experiencing, other relationships in the world of the patient. In other words, people alone do not change; systems change and on multiple levels. Perhaps a more felicitous way of stating this is that apparent change is reiterated or distributed throughout all systems and their respective constituents, just as those constituents support or are responsible for those changes in the first place. Here again, we see how complexity theory illuminates the vicissitudes of multiple experiential worlds. The distribution of change across the very systems that support it evolves in nonlinear ways and is influenced by the richness of the interactions. Seemingly small perturbations at the local level (say, the analytic relationship) can yield large effects in other localities within the larger system or systems, and vice versa. This sheds light on how a brief, apparently inconsequential comment from analyst to patient, for instance, can have profound consequences, whereas at times extravagant interventions and so-called provisions ultimately may have little impact.

This works on two levels of abstraction (our seventh attitude, making the "distinctions between dimensions of discourse—the *phenomenological* and the *explanatory/metaphysical*): Phenomenologically, we may *experience* others and ourselves as having changed, as being different from that with which we are familiar. On the explanatory level, we must understand change as always occurring across systems—the process whereby the constituents of multiple systems continually organize and reorganize into different patterns, perhaps like billiard balls whose positions in relation to one another are continually altered by the stroke of a cue. Change in one person, then, can be understood as an alteration in a complex system (with an indeterminate number of components) that is evidenced on the local level of the individual (e.g., the patient), much in the way that any psychological phenomenon (e.g., a dream, a fantasy, a feeling) that is said to occur *within* an individual is itself an emergent product and component of a larger system—something that is of *ambiguous ownership*. (Here again we witness the utility of Taylor's [2001] metaphors of two types of screens when reconceptualizing *the self*.) I believe *ambiguous ownership* is another term for what Cilliers (1998) refers to as "non-linear, distributed relationships between the constituents of the system" (p. 80). Therapeutic change in the patient, then, must be understood as an emergent property of a greater system, or multiple systems. In other words, when we speak of change occurring in one person, we create an artificial construct that necessarily disembeds that individual from her greater context. This is what traditional psychoanalytic doctrine has done to patients for decades. Instead, a nonlinear systems approach recognizes that the analytic dyad is shaped in part by historical though ongoing systems that are brought to the table by both patient and therapist. The emergent systemic properties of the analytic dyad then produce changes to what will become novel or modified systems—

changes in all the systems in which the patient is embedded, including those systems originally thought of as individual and historical and that continue to evolve in nonlinear ways.

In the next chapter, with this complexity sensibility in mind, let us explore in more depth the potential character, implications, and role of the analyst's attitudes in psychoanalysis and psychotherapy.

Notes

1 From *On the Road* by Jack Kerouac, copyright © 1955, 1957 by Jack Kerouac, renewed © 1983 by Stella Kerouac, renewed © 1985 by Stella Kerouac and Jan Kerouac. Used by permission of Viking Penguin, a division of Penguin Group (USA) Inc.

2 An attractor state, plainly stated, is a system's preference for a specific and identifiable arrangement of its components at a given point in time.

3 This is a must-read for anyone interested in the history and specifics of varying perspectives on therapeutic action. For further in depth study, see also Aron (2006); Cooper (2004); Fairburn (1958); Fosshage (2005); Friedman (1978, 2005); Gabbard and Westen (2003); Glover (1937); Greenberg (1981); Hoffman (1994); Kohut, (1982); Levenson (2003); Loewald (1960); Lyons-Ruth (1999); Mitchell (1997); Orange (2009); Preston (2008); Sandler (1976); Stern et al. (1998); Stolorow, Atwood, & Brandchaft (1994); and Stolorow et al. (2002).

Chapter 2

Attitudes

Attitudes are more important than facts.

—Karl A. Menninger[1]

[I]t is the attitude of the analyst toward the patient and toward the process that is most potent in whatever that change process may be.

—Estelle Shane[2]

In examining the therapeutic value of psychoanalytic complexity, I turn now specifically to the pivotal role of the therapist's attitudes. Such attitudes, often implicit and prereflective, exert powerful influences on the analyst, the patient, the treatment dyad, and the trajectory of the analytic relationship (Coburn 2007b, 2009; Frie & Coburn 2011). The patient's attitudes, of course, exert similar influences on the analyst, and what emerges ultimately is always a confluence of the multi-faceted and multi-determined attitudes of both parties.[3] A negotiation of their respective subjectivities (Pizer 1998)—including experiencing and living at the interface of their discrepant attitudes—informs the trajectory of the therapeutic relationship. You need look no further (but I recommend that you do) than the recent work of Hoffman (2009), Orange (2009), or Shane (2007) to grasp a palpable, contemporary sense of the central role personal attitudes play in therapeutic action. And if attitudes are "undeliberate interpretations," as Friedman (1982, p. 365) has averred, they most certainly are powerful determiners that shape the co-constituted trajectory of the relationship and the truths at which the analytic dyad arrives. Naturally, our attitudes inform our theory building and theory choices (Atwood & Stolorow 1979), just as our allegiances to specific theories, in turn, determine some of our clinical attitudes. (This is an instance of the action of feedback loops, or *recurrence*, a concept in complexity theory, to be discussed soon.) Many of our attitudes remain unformulated (Stern 1997) or within the realm of the unthought known (Bollas 1987). We hope to wrest them from the domain of the implicit, though we are not always successful. Nevertheless, their influence reverberates throughout our dyadic and socio-cultural-historical systems and beyond, and it behooves us, as clinicians, to examine their role in the treatment setting. Indeed, our attitudes about how things work, about how we relate in a particular dyad, become, over time, the subject matter of investigation and conscious elaboration by the analytic participants.

Attitude is at the core of any scientific, philosophical, artistic, or practical endeavor. Even the presumptions of neutrality and objectivity and the notion of suspending our presumably confounding attitudes, traditionally found in a variety of disciplines, are themselves attitudes that determine our approach and even alter the subject matter of investigation (Heisenberg 1958). The edict of *always look on the bright side of life* (the title of a song written and performed by Eric Idle that was featured in the 1979 film *Monty Python's Life of Brian*), for example, however dissociative or sardonic this advice may be, and having wound its way into a variety of pop psychology orientations, comprises one form of attitude. And, of course, privileging the role and influence of attitude in psychoanalysis and psychotherapy is an attitude in itself. There is no escape from where we stand. Stolorow and Jacobs (2006, p. 14) speak to the relentless context-embeddedness and omnipresence of our attitudes:

> Can interpretation ever be presuppositionless? We would answer, following Heidegger and his student, Gadamer, in the negative. Very briefly, according to Heidegger, interpretation is in every case grounded in a "fore-structure" (ibid., p. 194), which includes a guiding point of view or interpretive framework of "as's" that the interpreter brings to the act of interpretation. In virtue of this interpretive framework, interpretation, against Husserl, "… is never a presuppositionless apprehending of something presented to us" (ibid., pp. 191 ff.). …the essences of experience [thus] intuited could never be universal, necessary possessions a priori of a "pure cogito."

Indeed, there is no view from nowhere (Nagel 1986).

Another word for attitude (there are many of them) is *presupposition*, defined by the *Cambridge Dictionary of Philosophy* (Audi 1995) in the pragmatic sense as "what a speaker takes to be understood in making an assertion" (p. 641). What this definition does not include is that what a speaker takes to be understood is frequently not held in consciousness nor necessarily immediately grasped by the listener's consciousness. Presuppositions are often implicit. Some are dynamically unconscious—they may move in and out of awareness; and some are unvalidated—they may have never seen the light of day to begin with (Stolorow & Atwood 1996). Yet another word for attitude is *situatedness* (i.e., a situatedness in which our experiential worlds are not only shaped and informed by our socio-cultural-historical context [Frie 2011] but also ones in which we are consequently inclined in a specific manner relative to others or to other things). By analogy, we see this phenomenon in geometry or geology in which the subject matter of investigation frequently is lines and planes and their relationship to other lines and planes. A geometric plane is only relevant insofar as it stands in relation to another plane. Similarly, in writing about complexity and commenting on the deeper meaning of the word *relational*, Ghent (2002, p. 771) asserts:

> Notice the sentence [from Thelen and Smith, 1994, p. xix], "these solutions emerge from relations, not from design." It reminds me of "the words of the French mathematician, Henri Poincaré, the discoverer of what we now call chaos, that 'the aim of science is not things themselves, as the dogmatists in their simplicity assume, but the relations among things; outside these relations there is no reality knowable'" (Kelso, 1995, p. 97). To my mind it is in this meaning of relational, rather than its more superficial usage as the relations between people, that gives power and significance to the term relational psychoanalysis.

And I would add, outside the relationship between people's attitudes, the analyst's *and* the patient's, there is no conduit and trajectory for the reality that emerges and that we subsequently try to grasp.

Philosophers of mind speak of *propositional attitudes*, which refer to emotional postures that connect the person to a proposition—to what he or she thinks and states—and, effectively, the person to the world (Ramsey 1990). To posit a perspective about something also means to take a stand emotionally *about* that perspective. Linguistically, verbs reflect propositional attitudes:

> What sort of name shall we give to verbs like "believe" and "wish" and so forth? I should be inclined to call them "propositional verbs." This is merely a suggested name for convenience, because they are verbs which have the form of relating an object to a proposition. As I have been explaining, that is not what they really do, but it is convenient to call them propositional verbs. Of course you might call them "attitudes," but I should not like that because it is a psychological term, and although all the instances in our experience are psychological, there is no reason to suppose that all the verbs I am talking of are psychological.
>
> (Russell 1918, p. 227)

In contrast to Russell, I prefer the term *attitude* precisely because it *is* psychological.

In thinking of propositional attitudes, we also think of *direction of fit*, also a philosophy of mind concept (Searle & Vanderveken 1985). Essentially, a mind-to-world fit entails a *belief* about the world (or about another person), whether ultimately deemed true or otherwise. Conversely, a world-to-mind fit involves an *intention* or *desire* about the world, whether ultimately realizable or not. It bears emphasizing that these notions of *fittedness* hark back to a Cartesian worldview in which mind and world were considered disengaged and separate entities, which is anathema to a complexity sensibility. When an analyst says to her patient, "You feel responsible for all your woes," depending on her implicit attitude, she potentially combines both directions of fit into a single package. The implicit message might be, "I see you take full responsibility for all your problems, you feel you are the cause of all your woes, and I am suggesting that that may not be true, that there may be other factors out of your control" (the analyst's belief about the patient and the patient's world context—a mind-to-world fit); "I am also suggesting that it might be useful for you to consider that you are not entirely responsible for where you've arrived at and for the pain you are suffering" (the analyst's intention or desire for the patient—a world-to-mind fit). The presence of either one, or both, directions of fit can be found in virtually everything that gets said (or not said!). Propositional attitudes are everywhere; they are the fabric of human relating. Just as attitudes are "undeliberate interpretations" (Friedman 1982, p. 365), interpretations always carry with them undeliberate and sometimes deliberate attitudes.

Whereas the concept of attitude is multifaceted and can be defined in a variety of ways, I draw from Maduro (2011, personal communication, January 15) to offer one particularly cogent definition of attitude:

> A person's attitude in a given time and context is a manifestation of his subjectivity that entails a complex amalgamation of his beliefs, perceptual vantage-points, affective tilts, embodied countenance, behavioral shadows and styles, and other of his personal, subjective features. Further, this manifest subjective amalgamation—or attitude—is invariably conveyed, especially implicitly, to, and perceived to one degree or another by, others in the intersubjective field at hand and is imbued with a quality of credibility as perhaps the most reliable of all reflections of the person's subjectivity... As such, attitudes and the relational dynamics that they give rise to involve a complex, non-linear, highly impactful meaning-making process that can be emotionally healing or deleterious.

Note particularly Maduro's comment that an individual's underlying attitude "is imbued with a quality of credibility." This is exactly what gives attitudes—as distinct from conscious opinions or intellectual musings—their mutative power, partly because the recipient of an attitude (as I am using the term) is not left with a sense of being persuaded, taught, or coerced in any way, nor is she left with an absence of the feeling of honesty and sometimes conviction about what is being proffered. In some ways, they are more aligned conceptually with unintentional hints (Phillips 1999)—attitudes without a mission to change, persuade, or cajole. And, naturally, sometimes attitudes do have as their prime focus a mission to change but ideally not superseding the wish to inquire and understand. Another enticing definition of attitude is found in Piers's (2005, p. 251) description of the mind and its accompanying attitudes:

> I see the mind as a nonlinear system that arranges, coordinates, and organizes subjective experience—including the subjective experience of self—but

always does so from a set of predisposing attitudes. By attitude, I mean to suggest that the mind has a particular perspective or vantage point in relation to the flow of subjective experience, leaving it poised in a state of biased readiness to perceive, organize, interpret, respond to, and remember experience in a distinctive and recognizable manner.

Attitudes, as I think of them, are more akin to enduring squiggles (Winnicott 1971).

Importantly, I am not implying that the therapist's attitudes, however well-intentioned, complexity-informed, and potentially understated or implicit they may be, will not sometimes be *experienced* by the patient as persuasion or coercion or in some ways discrepant from that of the therapist's experiences and beliefs. We can never know how others ultimately will experience and assimilate our attitudes until it has happened in real time and then reflected upon. Intersubjective disjunctions (Stolorow & Atwood 1996), in which each party is experiencing the same psychological event in relatively dissimilar ways, abound, and it is incumbent upon the therapist to attune as much as possible to the ongoing interactions and reactions of the patient to any interpretive activity on the part of the therapist. Where any hint of coercion or even undesired persuasion on the part of the therapist, as experienced by the patient, emerges, a close and ongoing exploration remains an essential ingredient in any therapeutic system. That is also not to say that certain specific attitudes should not be conveyed with explicit, conscious passion. Hoffman's seminal 2009 article titled, *Therapeutic Passion in the Countertransference*, typifies this sensibility. He states that there is a "genre of literature (e.g., the work of Howard Levine 1994, 1999) that has continued in that spirit of recognition of the inevitability of influence [of the therapist] along with subtle depreciation of its constructive potentials" (p. 623). Of course, influence is central in psychoanalysis and psychotherapy, and it should be appreciated and valued, not depreciated. The simple (though it is not that simple) act of inquiry and exploration is, in itself, immensely influential.

Much has been written in psychoanalysis about explicit attitudes with which one should approach the clinical setting. Schafer's (1983) work offers but one example of the attention paid to explicit recommendations about essential attitudes in the psychoanalytic endeavor. Of course S. Freud (1912, 1913b) before him had elaborated similar objectivist/observer attitudes that were to guide the analyst, which included neutrality, anonymity, abstinence, and discipline. More recently, Lichtenberg et al. (1996) outlined ten guidelines describing how the analyst should approach the clinical setting, reflecting a notable instance of the conscious use and advantage of adopting certain attitudes. As a specific instance of the role of influential attitudes in psychoanalysis, I find compelling Aron's (1996) attitude that underlies his verbal self-disclosures. His *to the best of my knowledge* sensibility, embedded in his communications about how he experiences himself, perhaps in contrast to his patient's experience of him, always conveys that he (the analyst), too, has an unconscious and that the patient may be glimpsing something of that to which the analyst is not yet privy. This form of fallibilism (Orange 1995, 2006) reflects a powerful attitude that opens possibilities for expanding self-awareness and human relating. However, it does require a willingness to tolerate a healthy if painful dose of Cartesian anxiety (Bernstein 1983), including the unease of either not knowing and/or of knowing that an other might know something more about the one thing we would expect to have the best grasp of: our selves. Frank (1997) extends this sensibility in underscoring the attitude of a "willingness to be known" (p. 308) or discovered by our patients, in concert with our acceptance that, indeed, our patients know far more about us than we ourselves may know. Frank (2012) states: "it behooves us to open ourselves to the notion that our patients are indispensable collaborators who help us gain self-awareness" (p. 313). This is an instance of one among many influential attitudes that may serve to open up areas of investigation and relating that otherwise would remain closed to the therapeutic dyad.

Conversely, some attitudes—those linked to the incessant maintenance and protection of one's familiar sense of self and/or the rigid and relentless identification with key figures in one's life—can be coercive and corrosive, often leading to the constriction of our affective worlds and relational options. Phenomenologically, one instance of this phenomenon is reflected in the work of Benjamin (1998) and the concept of split complementarity in which one or both parties insist on having the upper hand in defining oneself and the other. Resonant with Benjamin, Davies (2003) states,

> cases of apparently inescapable therapeutic impasse always pose for me the dilemma that patient and analyst become prisoners of the coercive projective power of each other's vision; each becomes hopelessly defined by the other and incapable of escaping the force of the interactive pull to act in creative and fully agentic ways. Most problematic of all, I believe, is the collapse of a certain kind of potential countertransference space: a space in which the analyst's playful fantasies live and thrive; a place in which analytic fantasy and freedom can often give rise to creative flights and more hopeful responses that sidestep the deadening cycles of repetitive reenactment. (pp. 15–16)

Drawing from the spirit of Davies' clinical examples, a patient might state, "I want you to love me," but simply reading that in print, as you just have, does not really disclose the feeling, or attitude, encased in the proposition. The propositional attitude, linked to a world-to-mind fit (or in this instance, misfit), might be one of a demanding, aggressive desire that is not being fulfilled, in which case, depending on the analyst's response (e.g., defensive flight from deepening the engagement), the potential therapeutic play space collapses into the "deadening cycles of repetitive reenactment" of which Davies speaks. These types of attitudes, of which patients and analysts are both capable—imperious, demanding, and coercive—extract the vitality and dynamism out of any otherwise complex, dyadic system. Some attitudes are better than others when it comes to striving to keep a relationship dynamic, unpredictable, alive, energetic, and open to new possibilities.

Another vantage point from which to consider attitudes centers on the concept of markedness (Aron 2006; Benjamin 2004; Fonagy, Gergely, Jurist, & Target 2002). To extrapolate from the work of Aron (2006) and Benjamin (2004), our interventions, verbal or otherwise, are always necessarily *marked* or accompanied by an associated attitude, just as our *mirroring* responses always include aspects of our own subjectivity, are marked by them. This action not only allows for the potential of increasing one's sense of self/other delineation in the process of getting to know oneself through the mind of the other but also provides the underpinning for one coming to *know* the other, whether we like it or not. Aron states:

> Benjamin (2004a) illustrates [the] principle [of the symbolic third, allowing for self-other differentiation] by referring to the term "marking" or "marked response." The idea of markedness was originally developed by Gyorgy Gergely and is described by Fonagy et al. (2002) where they elaborate a social-biofeedback theory of affect-mirroring. Recent conceptualizations of "mirroring" emphasize that, no matter how well attuned a parent is to the infant's state, her mirroring facial and vocal behaviors never perfectly match the infant's behavioral expressions. Mothers, and other adults, "mark" their affect-mirroring displays (that is, they signify that these responses are reflections of the other's feelings rather than being expressions of their own feelings) by exaggerating some aspect of their own realistic response. The mother "marks" her mirroring response to her child to signal, so to speak, that it is her version of his response. ...The infant recognizes and uses this marked quality to "decouple" or to differentiate the perceived emotion from its referent (the parent) and to "anchor" or "own" the marked mirroring stimulus as expressing his or her own self-state. (pp. 357–358)

Analogously, *marking* our propositions—about which we have little choice in the moment—differentiates an otherwise objective and neutral proposition from our subjective feeling or stance vis-à-vis that proposition. Attitude can be thought of as a form of *markedness*—a feeling, stance, or impression about that which is being either mirrored or simply proposed.

Ferenczi (1928) was onto this when he spoke of empathy as part of a two-stage process: *Einfühlung* and *Abschätzung*—the former referring to an empathic process in which something of the other's emotional world is grasped and understood and the latter referencing the assessment and appraisal of that which was discerned through empathy, including, importantly, the communication of that assessment to the other, often in the form of an implicit attitude. There is no movement or expression without an accompanying attitude. We might say that all of our propositions or interpretations are *marked* by an attitude that reflects what we think and feel about what we say and do.

Clearly, attitudes are powerful and influential meta-messages that determine much of the trajectory of the therapeutic relationship: what will unfold and what will not. There are few arenas in which the influence of attitudes is more profoundly witnessed than in our perspectives about our personal subjectivities. Frank (2012) comments that

> we must strive, perhaps more conscientiously than ever before, to remain accountable for our own subjectivity, which rather than simply interfering "noise" has come to be seen as a source of information vital to our work and the process of healing. (p. 315)

Our attitudes toward human subjectivity (addressed at length in the next chapter) in psychoanalytic history have indeed evolved into more intelligent and clinically useful directions; the evolution of our countertransference literature since the early twentieth century (Bacal & Thomson 1996; Balint & Balint 1939; Epstein & Feiner 1979; S. Freud 1910a, 1910b, 1912, 1913b; Hoffman 2009; Little 1951; Orr 1954; Stern 1924 [just to name a few of hundreds]) interestingly reflects that evolution. This literature, slowly but surely, reflected an essential exploration of the impact of how we hold the idea and experience of our personal subjectivities. To our benefit, we have more recently arrived at the sense that our subjectivities, rather than being obstinate impediments to reason and sound clinical work, are pathways to insight and therapeutic action and deserve our central focus and respect.

Returning to Hoffman (2009) for a moment, he states that "the analyst has the power to inspire change in the patient through active imaginative involvement and the exercise of influence that often goes beyond interpretation although it certainly may include it" (p. 619). Here, I believe, he refers in part to the more explicit conveyance of the analyst's attitudes toward the patient's emotional world and her convictions about how she and the world work. He also substantiates the idea of the inevitability and ubiquity of the analyst's influence. He draws upon Buechler (2002) when he writes:

> Sandra Buechler (2002) in the context of conveying her sense of Eric Fromm's approach to psychoanalytic work, wrote:
> > The analyst's deepest convictions about life's meaning will shape every particle of his work, whether he wills it or not. To face this dilemma and to consciously bear that who we are will have this much impact can be frightening, confusing, and burdensome. …[and] the more we are willing to acknowledge our personal impact, the less we mystify the patient and force him to furtively glean who we are. We do not have a choice about having an impact. We only have a choice about whether to recognize it or not and *through a brave act of facing our responsibility* [italics added], grasp the courage to inspire. (p. 277)
>
> (Hoffman 2009, p. 623)

Indeed, it is this inspiration that many of our explicit and implicit attitudes can convey to our patients.

A closer examination of our personal attitudes specifically toward our subjectivity and their corresponding epistemological frameworks provides an illuminating instance of the influential role of implicit attitudes in psychoanalysis and psychotherapy, how they shape and inform the trajectory of the clinical relationship. Thus, before advancing to an exploration of complexity and complex systems (Chapter 4) and then on to an examination of complexity-informed attitudes (Chapter 5), this next chapter provides a useful example of the operation of attitudes in clinical work, prefiguring the central theme of this book: thinking about psychoanalytic complexity and examining the implications of the attitudes that emanate from such a sensibility.

Notes

1 Menninger, K. (1938) *Man Against Himself.* New York: Harcourt Brace, p. 143. Copyright © 1938 and renewed 1966 by Karl Menninger. Reprinted by permission of Houghton Mifflin Harcourt Publishing Company. All rights reserved.
2 Shane, E. (2009) 'My life with self psychology'. In N. Vanderheide & W. J. Coburn (eds.), *Self and Systems: Explorations in Contemporary Self Psychology.* Boston, MA: Blackwell, p. 236.
3 Arguably one of the distinctions between a patient and an analyst is that the analyst is principally concerned with the explicit examination of the patient's *and* the analyst's attitudes, including affective valence, underlying organizing themes, and relational proclivities, whereas the patient may not be so inclined, depending on the patient. The analyst invites the patient to be curious and to explore, and the patient may or may not accept her invitation. The self and motivational systems theory model (Lichtenberg et al. 1992) beautifully depicts the frequent disharmony inherent in two participants operating from discrepant motivational systems (e.g., the analyst wishes to be curious and to explore, whereas the patient may want attachment or sex or physical safety).

Chapter 3

Two Attitudes on Personal Subjectivity

Everyone and anyone is much more simply human than otherwise.

—Harry Stack Sullivan[1]

The continuing, overarching paradigm shift in psychoanalysis, as highlighted in the Introduction, directs our attention more than ever toward the intricacies of our personal subjectivity and their inevitable influence on others and the world (and, of course, vice versa). It invites us to examine even more closely our subjective worlds and the attitudes we hold about them. Our ongoing obsession with human subjectivity is nothing if not relentless. Our attitudes about our personal subjectivity fundamentally create and inform much of how we experience ourselves, our beliefs about what we do and what our patients do and, importantly, our sense of relative certainty and convictions vis-à-vis our patients and the truths we do arrive at collaboratively. The personal attitudes we hold toward our respective subjective worlds play a pivotal role in determining, among other events, how lightly, or tenaciously, we hold onto our own belief systems.

A closer examination of our attitudes toward our subjectivity and their epistemological frameworks helps illuminate how self-experience emerges and develops and ultimately how we react to and interact with our patients. Our attitudes also determine how we regard the experiences of certainty and conviction, how we respond to the feeling that we know something and that perhaps we are even wedded to knowing that something. Furthermore, these particular types of attitudes also shape and inform our perspectives regarding the breadth and vicissitudes of unconscious communication and other vital phenomena such as affect attunement (and misattunement), emotional resonance, and information transfer in general. Such an examination provides a useful example of how attitudes might operate among people and contribute to the unique directions relationships take. In particular, serving only as an initial and specific instance of thinking about the role of attitudes in psychoanalysis and psychotherapy, this chapter addresses the implications of assuming the relentless embeddedness of our subjective worlds in larger contexts from which we can never extricate ourselves (our second attitude). An alternative and contrasting attitude about how one might position one's personal subjectivity—what I refer to as *transcendence*—is juxtaposed here to *embeddedness* and explored with an eye on clinical situations that we clinicians face every day. Think of what follows as a thought experiment within our larger thought experiment.

Some speak of our subjectivity as an inescapable liability *and* asset; we are relegated to working with our limited, idiosyncratic perspectives. Whereas our necessarily delimited, subjective stances are perpetual and pervasive, they also serve as a powerful source of relational experiences that are intensely informative and developmental (Bollas 1987; Davies 2004; Ehrenberg 1992; Heimann 1950; Little 1951; Sandler 1976), and that evolve and expand through collaborative dialogue with the other (Lyons-Ruth 1999; Orange 1995, 2011). Our personal, biased, subjective experiences may provide, paradoxically, a potentially clearer window into how things are and how things work. Others consider it to be an inevitable, foreseeable, though mutable quality of humanness around which we need to work (Kohut 1984), but from which we are, with concerted effort and discipline, ultimately capable of extricating ourselves. This extrication is thought to lead to a more *objective* and *truer* view of our patients' emotional worlds. At the end of this spectrum resides the psychoanalytic objectivist who feels that she approaches the patient with a mental apparatus, akin to a laboratory instrument, that is capable of fundamentally clear, objective vision, hindered only by the occasional countertransference anomaly, the inevitable smudge on the microscope lens (Freud 1910b; Grotstein 1977, 2007; Kernberg 1976, 1984).

A rich example of one theorist who obviously gave much thought to this matter is Heinz Kohut. In his chapter titled "The Problem of Scientific Objectivity," from his seminal book, *How Does Analysis Cure?* (1984), Kohut invites us into his deliberations, and sometimes his equivocations, about the observer's access to objective reality, the analyst's penchant and striving for objective vision, juxtaposed with his subjectivity and its relative impact on what is being observed. He writes,

> Are there really truths of any significance and breadth that can be evaluated without regard to the observer who affirms them? Are there, in particular, psychological theories which, dealing with objectively ascertainable data, allow us to disregard the observing instrument, that is, the individuals who have formulated them and affirm their accuracy, relevance, and explanatory power? (p. 36).

One intriguing distinction (and possible conflation of two phenomena) only alluded to in this passage pertains to considering the impact of the observer on the observed. This can be, and in fact should be, conceptualized in two ways: first, that indeed the presence and unique character of the observer is helping shape and inform the object (or subject) of observation (today we generally take this assumption for granted); but second, that the subjective world of the observer is not solely impacting and shaping the observed but is, of course, also altering the observer's *experience* of the observed (the result of how the observer assimilates the observed). By *subjective*, or *subjective experience*, I refer, on one hand, to the characteristics of an experiential world that are fashioned by the peculiarities, idiosyncrasies, and uniqueness of the experiencing person *and* that of that person's surround. By *objective*, or *objective experience*, on the other hand, I reference the notion of a relatively clear and unfettered apprehension of what some have presumed to be an identifiable, external reality; in that light, an objective observer can be thought of essentially as empty random access memory (RAM) in a computer that then becomes populated by the same 0s and 1s that it is given, identical to those it observes on the outside. Philosophically, this has been referred to as the *correspondence theory of truth and reality*, dating back to Aristotle (i.e., a proposition is true if there is a fact that corresponds to it).[2]

Our personal attitudes toward our subjectivity contribute heavily to our creating and informing the subject matter of investigation, our *experience* of it and, ultimately, the manner in which we may hold our discoveries (e.g., as mutable and transforming or as bedrock, static truth). They determine which aspects of the patient's subjective world we choose to highlight and articulate or to ignore. They also inform to what degree we generate and sustain experiences of certainty and conviction and in what manner we will consequently interact with our patients. This chapter draws more needed attention to the idea that our personal experience of what is real and what is true is relentlessly context-dependent and context-sensitive. This idea is easily illustrated when we consider how what we record as experientially familiar, real, and true about ourselves in one setting can rapidly transform into something novel, surrealistic, uncertain, and perplexing in another.

Background

Traditionally rooted in an objectivist, one-person model science, psychoanalysis, psychology, psychotherapy, and their related fields have undergone a continuing paradigm shift over this last century, similar to transformations experienced by other seemingly unrelated fields. Resituating our notions of truth and reality, a variety of postmodern perspectives on truth and reality characterized this revolution, ultimately rejecting the notion of *the grand narrative* (Baudrillard 1994; Foucault 1977; Lyotard 1984). It engendered reconceptualizations about subjective experience and meaning-making and encouraged a greater openness to more dynamic, pluralistic, perspectival thinking (Aron 1996, 2006; Mitchell 1993, 2000). Orange (1995), for example, reviewed the development of psychoanalytic epistemology; she discussed and integrated notions of subjectivism, relativism, objectivism, and realism—each a salient view in its own right. She posited a synthesis of these perspectives, her idea of *perspectival realism*, in which "the real is an emergent, self-correcting process only partly accessible via personal subjectivity but increasingly understandable in communitarian dialogue" (p. 62).

Aron (1996), as another example, used the term *relational-perspectivism* in his linking "together the epistemological shift from positivism to constructivism and the shift within psychoanalytic metapsychology from the drive-discharge, energic, one-person model to the relational, or two-person, perspective" (p. 27). Stolorow (1997) went so far as considering distinctions between the one-person and two-person models as obsolete. He felt that nonlinear dynamic systems theory (Thelen & Smith 1994), another designation for complexity theory, contributed significantly to the revolution in paradigm (see Orange, Atwood, & Stolorow 1997), offering an invaluable metaphor for the psychoanalytic process. Shane et al. (1997) also invoked nonlinear dynamic systems theory as an integral component of their developmental systems self psychology model. Their innovative and highly integrative perspective remains a cogent example of the paradigm shift that we continue to witness in psychoanalysis and psychotherapy today. A few authors (e.g., Rabin 1995) addressed some of the practical implications of these alternative perspectives for practicing therapists: how we might behave differently with our patients, how we might feel different in the context of treatment, how our assumptions about what is going on interpersonally might change our experience of ourselves and our patients, and how we and our patients might thereby be affected.

Intersubjective systems theory and relational theory contributed heavily to the rethinking of etiology and epistemology. The development of these and related approaches, many of which kept in mind the mutual and reciprocal influences of both analyst and patient, had various precursors. One such precursor was the borrowing from physics of the notion of complementarity (Bohr 1963) and the principle of indeterminacy (Heisenberg 1958)—what was suggested in Sullivan's (1962) notion of participant-observation. Sucharov (1994) explored the impact of these perspectives, derived primarily from quantum physics. Infant research also contributed heavily, and continues rigorously to do so, to the reconceptualization of psychoanalytic etiology and epistemology (Beebe 2004, 2005; Beebe & Lachmann 1994; D. N. Stern 1985; Trevarthen 1979; Tronick 1989). These ideas not only highlighted the uniqueness, limitations, and advantages of the subjective observer but underscored concepts such as the *intersubjective field* (Stolorow, Brandchaft, & Atwood 1987) and the conceptually contrasting *analytic third* (Ogden 1994), in which "the interaction between observer and observed forms an intrinsic feature of the [relationship] phenomenon" (Sucharov 1994, p. 188) and, of great importance, in which the line of demarcation between the observer and the observed can only be arbitrarily, though meaningfully, chosen. The work of Winnicott (1953, 1965) helped set the stage for the recognition and use of this dimension of indeterminacy and *transitional space* shared by analyst and analysand.

Subjectivity

Central to many of our contemporary paradigms is the problem, and arguably the solution, of subjectivity—that of the patient and, more recently (in the last seventy-five years or so) that of the analyst. The patient's view of himself and the world, presumably emanating principally from what has been thought of as emotional disorder, had always been conceptualized as subjective if not distorted, delusional, transference-based, or in some fashion inconsistent with presumed, objective truth. This perspective is consistent with traditional science, scientism, and objectivist notions of reality—the zeitgeist in which Freud and many others evolved professionally. Indeed, the concept of transference ultimately had everything to do with the action of intrapsychic processes distorting an otherwise known and accessible external reality; said reality was rendered distorted via mechanisms such as regression, displacement, projection, or generally the alteration of what otherwise was, presumably, clearly right in front of you—in a word, a "false connection" (Freud 1893, p. 302). One's view of the analyst, if at all discrepant from that of the analyst herself, was considered an instance of wrenching reality into something it wasn't. And the analyst's job was to point this out and correct the distortions. Some did this with aplomb and elegance and others with authority and aggression. Alternatively stated, in some circles, transference existed essentially whenever the patient's perspective differed from that of the analyst!

In our more contemporary climate of the last fifty years or so, however, the patient's subjectivity has been much more considered and respected, and the analyst's subjectivity and its impact on the patient have been more seriously reconceptualized. From a contemporary viewpoint, it is not solely that the analyst's perspective about what is real and true is informed by his unique, preconfigured organizing principles (Stolorow et al. 1987) and his unique relational proclivities, but we assume now that the analyst's resulting percepts and experiences have, in turn, a compelling impact on the perceptual configurations of the patient (Mitchell 1993)—and vice versa. The Balints (1939) were onto this when they wrote about how the countertransference of the analyst may actually be informing and influencing the transference of the patient. Quite remarkable for 1939! Infant research has by now provided us with substantial research and compelling clinical data that point to our natural, human tendency toward reciprocal and mutual psycho-physiological influence shared by two or more individuals (Ainsworth & Bell 1974; Beebe 2004; Beebe & Lachmann 1994; Bowlby 1969, 1973, 1980; Main, Kaplan, & Cassidy 1985; D. N. Stern 1985, 2004; Tronick 1989; and many others).[3]

Some authors feel that the analyst's subjectivity essentially determines a great deal of the ultimate shape and character of the patient's analysis. As alluded to previously, the Balints anticipated this in their 1939 article in which they consider "whether transference is brought about by the patient alone, or whether the behavior of the analyst may have a part in it too" (p. 223). We realize now, of course, that indeed it does. Even contemporary fiction writers have acknowledged the analyst's essential contribution to the clinical exchange: "The true story of a therapeutic exchange begins not with the patient's present problem but with the healer's past" (Yglesias 1996, p. 9). Kohut (1984) states that the analyst "acknowledges [ideally] his own impact on the field he observes and, through such acknowledgment, broadens his perception of the patient" (p. 111). Cooper (1996) underscores this: "The choice of where to begin to formulate and what to interpret, as well as the goals of analysis, are the most visible expression of the analyst's subjectivity" (p. 265). From the standpoint of subject-centered and other-centered listening perspectives, Fosshage (1992, 2003) makes explicit the powerful impact of the analyst's subjectivity. He underscores that

> [a]lthough this listening stance [from within the analysand's vantage point] is designed "to hear" as well as possible from within the vantage point of the analysand, this is clearly a relative matter, for what is heard is always variably shaped by the analyst.
>
> (Fosshage 1992, p. 22)

The analyst's experience of the patient, even while listening through the *empathic mode of perception* (Kohut 1959, 1984; Lichtenberg et al. 1996), contains in it artifacts of the analyst's subjectivity.

Many contemporary analysts not only increasingly attempt to account for the inevitable impact of their subjectivity on the patient but feel that it may be exactly the conveyance of this subjectivity that is facilitative and constitutive for the patient. Personal attitudes abound and are the media of interpersonal exchanges and therapeutic action. Aron (1996) states, for example, that "not only does every intervention reflect the analyst's subjectivity, but it is precisely the personal elements contained in the intervention that are most responsible for its therapeutic impact" (p. 93). I have discussed elsewhere (Coburn 2001a) that it is precisely our human subjectivity that facilitates essential, shared experiences of *realness* between patient and analyst—what Stolorow and Atwood (1992) refer to as the *sense of the real* (not to be confused with the notion of reality testing)— and that these experiences are responsible for much of what is therapeutic in the psychoanalytic relationship.

Our subjectivity is shaped and informed by the very attitudes that are derived from it. Each at once affects and is affected by the other. This contention relates to our fourth attitude regarding the action of autocatalysm and recurrence. The idea that our underlying theoretical assumptions directly impact how we organize our perceptions, and ultimately how we will be with our patients, is not new. Wolf (1983) examines how theory informs the character and direction of our countertransference. Also, in his discussion of the liberating effects of the paradigm shift on analysts, Rabin (1995) highlights the impact theory always has on the practitioner:

each theory brings with it a greater probability of certain kinds of clinical errors, although it is excruciatingly difficult for many of us to appreciate the errors that are more intrinsic to the approach to which we are deeply committed. (p. 476)

Furthermore, Cooper (1996) expands on the powerful impact of our subjectivity and our theory, noting how subjectivity, theory, and practitioner are inextricably bound. Friedman (1988) has gone so far as suggesting that "[p]sychotherapy is a relationship interfered with by theory" (p. 1). Whether viewed as interfering or as facilitative, the therapeutic milieu is inextricably tied to our subjective stances: Mayer (1996) emphasizes that "the observer's point of view is necessarily part of what we are examining whenever we examine clinical facts" (pp. 715–716). From a reverse vantage point, Atwood and Stolorow (1979), and Stolorow and Atwood (1993) discuss at length the impact one's history and subjective experience have on one's theory-building and theoretical stance and consequently how one will work with patients. They clarify how the most powerful source of various theorists' psychological doctrines

can be found in the subjective experiential worlds of the personality theorists themselves…The subjective world of the theorist is inevitably translated into his metapsychological conceptions and hypotheses regarding human nature, limiting the generality of his theoretical constructions and lending them a coloration expressive of his personal existence as an individual. (p. 5)

Cooper (1996) echoes this sentiment when he states, "'theory' expresses our implicit or explicit technical stance, our views of therapeutic action, in sum, our subjectivity" (p. 256). Just as one's personal history and previous subjective experience create and inform one's theoretical constructions and one's countertransference (Atwood & Stolorow 1993), one's evolving attitudes toward one's subjectivity, at once stemming from and contributing to it, help determine the perceptual and relational configurations that coalesce in the patient-analyst relationship. Our attitudes toward our subjectivity help structure how we experience ourselves (e.g., what it feels like to hold and use our belief system), how we interpret our countertransference, and how we affect the patient.

Our Attitudes toward Our Subjectivity

The idea of the analyst's relative *embeddedness in* or *freedom from* his subjectivity occupies a vital position when examining potential attitudes toward one's own subjectivity. We can examine these dimensions of our subjectivity as we view its impact on our self-experience and, ultimately, on our patients' experience. In the interest of play, experimentation, and example, I delineate two essential types of attitudes toward one's subjectivity, referred to in this chapter as *embeddedness* and *transcendence*. Although there is a wide range of diverse attitudes toward one's subjectivity from which to choose, particularly illuminating is the dichotomy of the presumptions of *embeddedness in* or *freedom from* one's subjectivity—clearly of historical interest and controversy. In our thought experiment, we can consider that they represent the poles of a continuum on which our attitudinal organizing themes can potentially be plotted. I have chosen these concepts for the purpose of providing an entry point into thinking, later on more comprehensively, about the action of attitudes in the clinical setting.

Embeddedness

The attitude of embeddedness—in the Introduction referred to as the presumption of "our relentless embeddedness in contexts from which we can never extricate ourselves" (our second attitude)—assumes the inevitability and inextricability of one's subjective state. We are necessarily subjective, despite our penchant for measurement, replication, and common scientific languages. Even the subject matter of scientific inquiry, for many, is relentlessly subjectivity-infused. Mayer (1996) points out "that our work [while scientific] is quintessentially subjective and intersubjective" (p. 712). According to Renik (as cited in Mayer 1996), what actually characterizes science is "rigorous method. We can be scientific… if we acknowledge our subjectivity as clinician observers" (p. 712). The nature of this embeddedness is not limited by the invariance of one's organizing principles; one's subjectivity can be broadened and expanded through the development of newer organizing principles (Stolorow & Atwood 1996) and more adaptive, contemporary ways of relating. It can be expanded through relationally bringing to life the potential multiplicity of self-experience (Bromberg 2001, 2006; Davies 2004, 2005). And it can be reconceptualized by coming to sense that all experience is the result of interpretive activity (Gentile 2007, 2008, 2010), as opposed to simply and objectively observing the *brute facts* of the world (Holt 2012)—the presumed clarity and simplicity of the 0s and 1s alluded to earlier. We remain necessarily subjective and bound by our humanness. Sullivan (1962) emphasizes that "[t]his fundamental entity, this mind, can never effect its own apotheosis, be its verbal fog ever so dense, be its 'logic' ever so shiftily propagandistic. No mind can exteriorize itself for complaisant meditation about less transcendent minds" (p. 259). And no mind can observe the world, however seemingly unobtrusively, without impacting and helping shape it.

Questions of subjectivity, or objectivity for that matter, vis-à-vis ideas about truth and reality naturally stimulate epistemological concerns about one's experience of certainty and conviction about our patients and ourselves. The experience of certainty and conviction about something inclines us to claim knowledge of it and then to justify it. After all, from one perspective, we sit with our patients to generate insight and engagement, to increase our knowledge of the patient's subjective world, to stimulate constitutive and mutative experiences, to expand our respective experiential worlds, and, in general, to learn, develop, and play. Sometimes, this includes increasing our sense of certainty, and perhaps conviction, about phenomena pertaining to the self, or selfhood, the other, and the relational configurations between the two. Our purpose generally is not to encourage in our patients a sense of ongoing perplexity, confusion, and befuddlement, though helping ourselves and certain patients to develop the capacity to tolerate these states is vital to our continued progress. We want to learn, we want to know, and we want to feel we know. Essential to all biological life is the propensity to discern, assess, organize, make sense, and arrive at conclusions. Tolerating uncertainty and perplexity is difficult, to say the least; it runs counter to our essential humanness.

Despite this penchant for wanting to know and to keep hold of what we know, conveying a sense of certainty and conviction to the patient *about* the patient in some contexts subverts needed, continuing reorganization of the patient's developing sense of what feels right or clear about her own self-experience. In a given intersubjective context, depending on the foreground experience of the patient, it may be exactly a sense of uncertainty about herself, for example, that the patient may benefit from experiencing with her analyst. The patient may need to sense a capacity and willingness in the analyst to tolerate not knowing and to delay the formulation of conviction in favor of play and ambiguity. This may be what is constitutive and transformative for the patient at this point in time (Bacal 2011; Bacal & Carlton 2010)—that is, to allow continued transitional space and play (Winnicott 1971) via suspension of knowledge, certainty, and conviction. An attitude of embeddedness about one's subjectivity might help facilitate this experience between patient and analyst, as play, ambiguity, and uncertainty are perhaps more concordant with the analyst's self-experience, and this may be more developmentally helpful with certain patients in certain contexts.

I do not suggest that an analyst with an *embeddedness* attitude would not experience a sense of truth, reality, and conviction about the patient. As Aron (1996) states, "an analyst may interpret with a sense of conviction even while eschewing certainty and abandoning positivist epistemological presuppositions" (p. 94). This is a way of conceptualizing what Cooper (1996) refers to as the "impermanence of a clinical fact" (p. 258). The analyst's subjectivity in some contexts may facilitate knowledge and conviction about the patient and help provide what is constitutive for the patient, as alluded to previously. This sensibility is resonant with Orange's (2011) attitudes of fallibilism and the hermeneutics of trust. That analyst would be more inclined toward, in Aron's (1996) words, "deconstructing whatever storylines our patients present to us or that we have constructed with them so that we and they do not become rigidly fixated to any one narrative construction" (pp. 262–263). Alternatively stated, this reflects an attitude of "recognizing that what we 'know' or understand is inevitably partial and often mistaken" (Orange 1995, p. 43). Stimulating a Cartesian anxiety (Bernstein 1983), or the "fear of structureless chaos" (Stolorow 1994, p. 203), in the patient could or could not be reparative and constitutive for the patient, and it is left to the analyst and patient to explore and make determinations about this when it is felt to be temporally and contextually relevant and useful to do so.

Transcendence

This particular attitude toward one's personal subjectivity—one *not* derived from a complexity sensibility—inclines one to feel that one can know and assume something about the patient, something that is presumed to be real and true, via shedding one's idiosyncratic, subjective perspective. It can potentially position *the truth* and *the understood* in a less-than-dynamic and emergent framework. It can generate and help maintain a sense of certainty and conviction about the patient, for the therapist and perhaps for the patient, which may or may not be useful. This can be anxiety-reducing, can provide a sense of accomplishment, and can sometimes even be transformative and constitutive for the patient, depending on the current requirements and organization of the patient's emotional world.

This stance implies that though one's organizing principles generally tend to shape and inform one's perspectives, once analyzed, they may be placed aside to capture a clear, *objective* perspective of what is being examined and explored (e.g., the patient, the patient's response to the analyst, and the relational field), as if aspects of our subjectivity, once accounted for, no longer influence the clinical relationship. It is loosely akin to an aspect of subjectivity discussed by Slochower (1996). In her discussion of the analyst's holding function in relation to her subjectivity, she acknowledges the "centrality of the analyst's subjectivity in the therapeutic process" (p. 323). She speaks of the analyst's subjectivity, however, as something from which she may protect "the hyperalert patient" through choosing "to hold" (p. 326). She feels that the analyst is capable of "suspend[ing] her own subjectivity when it is discrepant with this experience [i.e., the experience of the patient creating and destroying the 'analyst-mother' at will, in the Winnicottian sense]" (p. 327). Later, Slochower suggests that the analyst is capable of "temporarily set[ting] aside or protect[ing] the patient from her own [the analyst's] subjectivity" (p. 328). And in some respects, this is clinically achievable and sometimes necessary. As clinicians, we frequently are deciding what to share and perhaps what to withhold in the way of specific information, depending on the context in the moment. The more extreme version of this presumption, however—that we can acknowledge our subjectivity, account for it, and then place it in some sort of suspension, out of the patient's awareness—reflects what I mean by the transcendence attitude toward one's subjectivity. I am reminded here of the ubiquity of the mutual and reciprocal unconscious communication processes that continually unfold between two or more individuals and of how knowledge of these processes challenges our presumed capacity to cloak or otherwise set aside our personal subjectivities and subjective states.

The transcendence standpoint, applied differently, reflects Kohut's (1984) specific attitude toward countertransference and the obstructing influence of it on the analyst as an *observing instrument*. He states that:

[i]f we want to see clearly, we must keep the lenses of our magnifying glasses clean; we must, in particular, recognize our countertransference and thus minimize the influence of factors that distort our perception of the analysand's communications of his personality. (p. 37)

In that sense, the cleaner the lens, the more clearly we may grasp the *reality* of the patient's experience. Aside from this particular facet of Kohut's sensibility, however, he technically could otherwise be positioned in the *embeddedness* stance, insofar as he was deeply aware of the necessity of not holding presumptions about the patient and of attempting to listen closely to what the patient felt was *true*. Recall his oft-quoted admission that

> [i]f there is one lesson that I have learned during my life as an analyst, it is the lesson that what my patients tell me is likely to be true—that many times when I believed that I was right and my patients were wrong, it turned out, though often only after a prolonged search, that *my* rightness was superficial whereas *their* rightness was profound. (pp. 93–94)

Freud's (1937) empirical approach exemplifies the more polarized version of the transcendence perspective, substantially illustrated in *Analysis Terminable and Interminable*:

> [the analyst] must possess some kind of superiority, so that in certain analytic situations he can act as a model for his patient and in others as a teacher. And finally we must not forget that the analytic relationship is based on a love of truth. (p. 248)[4]

Here, consistent with an archeological model, truth is not only objective and uncoverable, and once uncovered, static, but requires conviction to propel it into the mind of the patient. Note Freud's (1910a) emphasis on how "one of the necessary preliminaries to the treatment" involves "informing the patient of what he does not know" (p. 225).

This attitude may engender in us a degree of certainty and conviction about the patient that potentially acts as a coercive agent directed at the patient, encouraging or supporting compliance, accommodation (Brandchaft 2007), pseudo-health, and/or variations of what historically has been referred to as *transference cure* (Freud 1913b; Dysart 1977). At the least, if an analyst should arrive at a point of certainty, and perhaps conviction, about an aspect of the patient and chooses not to "induce [the patient] to remember something that has been experienced by him and repressed" (Freud 1937, p. 258), his withheld, *objective* opinions about the patient may nonetheless affect the patient via unconscious communications that occur on a millisecond-by-millisecond basis. This can occur despite the analyst's open invitations to the patient for continued exploration. The transcendence attitude runs completely counter to a psychoanalytic complexity sensibility.

Attitudes in Action

The following clinical story illustrates a predominantly transcendence perspective, or attitude, with occasional facets otherwise found in the embeddedness stance. This particular vignette is one in which the analyst's specific attitude appears to be at cross-purposes with what might otherwise be mutative for his patient.[5]

Dr. Sam's attitude toward his own subjectivity was varied. He accepted that although he was essentially tied to his own organizing principles and perceptions, he also felt that he was receptive to the affective and cognitive states of his patients. He believed he potentially had a direct, unfettered link to the psyches and experiences of his patients, and this link was accomplished and maintained through the medium of intellect, emotional resonance, and projective identification. Dr. Sam thought of projective identification as the process whereby a patient disavows or dissociates potential affective experience, including the mechanisms whereby such affective experience might be defended against, by projecting it onto or into the analyst and then somehow stimulating in the analyst the experience of the projected thoughts and feelings. Once stimulated, the analyst may then identify with that material originating in the patient and therefrom experience a disavowed aspect of the patient's psyche. This would occur apart from the influence of Dr. Sam's subjective perspective. Dr. Sam's invocation of the projective identification concept,[6] presumed outright in the absence of playing with uncertainty and with a *hermeneutics of trust* (Orange 2011) collaboration with the patient, exemplifies an instance of the transcendence perspective. This was Dr. Sam's attitude toward his own subjectivity and his potential for true, objective vision.

John's (the patient's) attitude toward his own subjectivity, alternatively, was more embeddedness-oriented. In many instances, he held his beliefs and convictions about the world rather lightly and often felt he would most likely never attain a clear, objective view of events, such as how others experience him. His perspective seemed to be less a function of any philosophical regard for an entrenchment in one's subjective perspective, arrived at via intensive self-reflection, but rather arising more from not having originally experienced an affectively clear, consistent, and responsive caregiver surround.[7] As a result, John had not attained a sense of clarity and certainty about his subjective experience and perspective (a *sense of the real*), especially in terms of how he affected others emotionally. He often withdrew from interpersonal exchanges, feeling bewildered, unclear, and perplexed. His experience of others and the world in general as true and real was tenuous and derived primarily from a physically unavailable father and an affectively disorganized mother, whose debilitating problems with self-regulation occupied her own mind most of the time. Much of John's experience of her centered on a sense of emotional disconnection and sleepiness. This was particularly evident when his mother was intoxicated, which she often was. John felt this to be an affectively dangerous and disorganizing situation and would often respond with a dissociation of his needs and longings for care, attention, and valuing by an other and ultimately with an interpersonal withdrawal of his own.

In most of his sessions with John over a three-month period, Dr. Sam continually experienced an undeniable sensation of being drugged, sleepy, and perplexed. This self-experience was at times quite overpowering. He thought this was something that most therapists felt at one time or another. On the basis of Dr. Sam's knowledge of John's history with his alcoholic and abusive mother and his patient's proclivity toward what seemed to him like affectively sterile communications, Dr. Sam believed that his self-experience of anesthesia and interpersonal distance evolved directly from a form of projective identification and perhaps from other forms of affect contagion. On one particular day, Dr. Sam escorted John into his office and braced himself for what he anticipated to be yet another onslaught of somnambulism and anesthesia from his patient. To Dr. Sam's surprise, which he kept to himself, John seemed amazingly awake and accessible. Dr. Sam thought,

> He is struggling to hide something. He is concerned that if he continues to make me sleepy and drugged, as he has been recently, I will tire of him, and he will lose me. He is trying to be cheerful.

Dr. Sam nevertheless readied himself for heavy eyelids and another difficult session.

"How are you today," John said.

"Fine thanks, and you?" Dr. Sam replied.

"All right, I guess," John said. "A bit apprehensive about a repeat of last session."

"What about our last session, exactly?"

"Oh, you know, how I made you feel so drugged, and how I was drugging myself to escape my feelings, I suppose." [John's phrase, "I suppose," does not draw Dr. Sam's attention here.]

"Yes, well, I think you did have rather strong feelings, and we've come to know how painful they are to actually experience and talk about." [Dr. Sam here is feeling rather affectively restricted in preparation for his patient's anesthesia, but is also curious and inquisitive about his patient's emotional experience. Dr. Sam does not inquire about how John experienced him in their last session or in the present.]

John begins to appear sleepy, stating, "Yeah, I can feel it coming on already." [This seems to be of no surprise to either person.]

"Any ideas what brings this on at this moment?"

"Well," John said, "no, but I was just thinking about my mother and her being so out of it so much of the time. I remember when my Dad would be gone a lot and my Mom would just drink and smoke all the time. I would just space out in my room, I guess."

"Yes, and I think you continue to give me a good sense of what it was like for you—with all the drugging, sleepiness, and withdrawal—trying to deal with your mother's absence. Perhaps you anticipate my absenting myself, instead of remaining in contact with you." [Dr. Sam reestablishes here his own sense of certainty and does not make a mental or verbal note of John's lack of certainty (potentially noted in his concluding phrase, "I guess").]

"I'm sorry, it's hit again. I just can't stand this sleepiness. And now I'll probably drag you down with me." [John assumes here a more subordinate position and accepts, apologetically, that he is the perpetrator of the anesthetic experience. This proves to be another repetitive experience for John. Dr. Sam feels a stronger sense of conviction here about John and his dynamics surrounding the sleepiness.]

This clinical snapshot, reflecting Dr. Sam's assumption that his self-experience was exclusively a product of John's psyche, led Dr. Sam to conclusions about his patient and his patient's fears and not necessarily about himself and his relationship with John. He did not interpret his own anesthesia experience as his unique response, such as, perhaps, a narcissistic injury in response to John's pattern of relating or, perhaps, a response to an admixture of intersecting personalities. Dr. Sam conceptualized that he had been used as a receptacle for and metabolizer of John's disavowed affect, as well as for John's dissociative mechanisms, much in the way a Petri dish might be used for cultivating bacteria. This was distinct from conceptualizing his experience as a bidirectional, relational event between two people, such as affect attunement or a form of mutual regulation.

The content of Dr. Sam's attitude—that his subjectivity is present but mutable and subject to transcendence—helped define his anesthesia experience with John; it inclined Dr. Sam to view his own emotional absence as the borrowed property of his patient and as the logical outcome of his patient's history of abuse, numbness, and dissociation. Dr. Sam's perspective caused him to focus predominantly on the defensive characteristics of his patient vis-à-vis his patient's history and the anxiety usually presumed to exist beneath states of disorganization and dissociation. Dr. Sam concluded that the function of similar but separate experiences of dissociation in each was principally to provide insight into John's history, into how he continued to block possible transference feelings, and into what could be a much more colorful and adaptive affective life. Dr. Sam believed that John unconsciously intended Dr. Sam to experience the drugged state of mind so that he might better grasp John's own experience. Within this framework, Dr. Sam did not consider that the dissociative anesthesia he was experiencing from his patient was perhaps not exactly consistent with his patient's experience or that his patient's state was a direct response to an emotional state within the analyst (i.e., to the contribution of the analyst). He felt that his own subjective stance did not preclude a direct, objective access to affective states and defense mechanisms in his patient.

Dr. Sam's specific attitude toward his subjectivity vis-à-vis his patient in this vignette not only informs how he experiences himself but determines his level of conviction about what is true and real about his patient. His sense of certainty and conviction could have a positive impact on his patient, or it could be less than useful. Dr. Sam's certainty about the origin and ownership of his patient's *projective material*, for example, the experience of anesthesia, conveys a message of certainty and clarity of knowledge about his patient's state of mind and perhaps even its etiology. This could potentially be a facilitative and constitutive experience for his patient—that his patient is being noticed and responded to with certainty and conviction. Despite his apparent sense of open-mindedness and exploratory freedom, Dr. Sam does remain inwardly persuaded by what he feels is an objective truth about his patient. This he cannot help but convey to his patient in an unconscious if not conscious manner and, in fact, Dr. Sam may deem it developmentally helpful to do so. Here, the potential for realizing a developmental advantage, however, hinges on whether Dr. Sam's *certainty and clarity of knowledge* actually correspond with his patient's experience and emotional meanings. And in this case, it does not, as evidenced by his patient's anesthetic withdrawal and subordination to the analyst's perspective. In this context, the felt conviction of the analyst could be an invitation for patient compliance and, potentially, a foreclosure of any further, genuine exploration by his patient into the meaning of what looks like dissociation. As he necessarily did in the past, John must isolate and sequester, once again, what otherwise could be an expansion and continued definition of his own selfhood through a continued, mutual, albeit ambiguous, exploration of selfhood and otherhood in relationship.

In this specific exchange, John experienced Dr. Sam's own anesthesia experience as both an affective withdrawal and detachment, similar to his mother's response to John's attempts at deriving emotional contact and at organizing his own internal world. Partly in response to Dr. Sam's unconsciously conveyed sense of conviction about his patient's state of mind, perhaps John experienced Dr. Sam as clearly delineating what John's subjective world must be like, as opposed to feeling invited to join in a mutual, shared struggle to ascertain his experience firsthand in a collaborative fashion. A developmental need and longing were missed, and the process of a defensive disavowal was bolstered.

It is important to note that this was not a situation in which Dr. Sam spoke self-assuredly as determiner and arbiter of the truth about John. Dr. Sam had verbally invited John to share in a mutual exploration of his impressions and associations regarding his own felt experience. Dr. Sam had, by most standards, provided John with an atmosphere of self- and mutual discovery and of exploratory freedom. It was, however, Dr. Sam's essential experience of himself as certain, his attitude about his *knowledge* of his patient, gathered independently and unidirectionally from his patient, and his attitude toward his capacity to transcend his subjectivity, that ultimately facilitated an unconsciously conveyed sense of certainty and conviction about his patient to his patient.

Ultimately, Dr. Sam and his patient loosened and unraveled their intersubjective disjunction through a gradual, thorough investigation of their discrepant, subjective perspectives and concomitant experiences of each other. It was primarily Dr. Sam's eventual shifting of his attitude of transcendence, through continued self-reflection, toward a more embeddedness-oriented stance that facilitated a development away from what had become a familiar, repetitive enactment for this particular analytic dyad. This is not to devalue the experience and communication of certainty and conviction in this or any other context, even though at times they may be highly discrepant with or even antithetical to the type of affective responsiveness most useful to the patient at the time. Instead, it calls to task the way in which one might potentially arrive at the personal experience of certainty and conviction vis-à-vis the patient, that is, via the attitude of transcendence.

The centrality and relevance of the analyst's subjectivity in the analytic context compel us to examine more closely the extent of its impact on our patients and on us. In this chapter, I have highlighted the impact one's attitude—in particular, toward one's subjectivity—has on one's experience of selfhood and one's sense of certainty and convictions about the patient and our shared world. The two specific attitudes explicated here serve as an experimental threshold into understanding the enormous impact attitudes have on the clinical surround in general. Next, we turn to some of the basic concepts complexity theory invites us to consider, and then, in Chapter 5, to an exploration of a much broader range of attitudes, including their clinical implications, that emanate from such a sensibility.

Notes

1 From Henry Stack Sullivan (1953) *The Interpersonal Theory of Psychiatry*, New York: W.W. Norton, p. 32. Copyright © 1953 by the William Alanson White Psychiatric Foundation. Used by permission of W.W. Norton & Company, Inc.

2 See Orange (2002) for a thorough exploration of and discussion regarding the traditional notion of the dichotomy of inside/outside and its implications for clinical practice.

3 See Seligman (2012) for a thorough and cogent explication of the relevance and impact of developmental research on our current clinical sensibilities.

4 Unfortunately, often it was the analyst's truth and not the patient's that got loved.

5 I am grateful to Dr. Sam, the analyst in this vignette, for communicating to me the ultimate development of, and insight into, the experiences of both analyst and patient in this specific example.

6 For an overview of the development of the concept of projective identification, see Klein (1946); Bion (1952; 1959); Grinberg (1962); Malin (1966); Ogden (1979); Renik (1980); Tansey and Burke (1985); Kernberg (1987); Field (1991); Grotstein (1995, 2007); Seligman (1999); Mills (2000); and Mendelsohn (2011).

7 It is vital to distinguish between states of uncertainty and perplexity that are grounded in an archaic deficit in the capacity for a *sense of the real* (Coburn 2001a)—a deficit in the capacity for feeling relatively clear and certain about one's perceptions, impressions, and general emotional experiences—resulting from an invalidating surround, as opposed to those states emerging from intentional and practical suspension of presumed knowledge and belief in the service of further dialogue and exploration.

Chapter 4

Complexity Theory and Emotional Life

All things (including those that come at last to triumph mightily) are at their beginnings so small and faint in outline that one cannot easily convince oneself that from them will grow matters of great moment.

—Matteo Ricci[1]

Ceaselessly the philosopher finds himself obliged to reinspect and redefine the most-grounded notions, to create new ones, with new words to designate them, to undertake a true reform...

—Maurice Merleau-Ponty[2]

Our minds are open systems embedded in an interactive matrix with other minds.

—Stephen Mitchell[3]

Often, new lenses are disconcerting when you first try them on. The world seems too blurry, too clear, too distorted, or perhaps too frightening. For many of us, trying on a complexity theory lens, clinically or otherwise, is no exception. For me, it has been exciting, mind-altering, sometimes perplexing, sometimes unnerving, and at moments, frankly, rather frightening. To think of the human and non-human systems through which we perpetually move and make our respective ways as truly that dynamic, messy, and anarchistic—in contrast to their superficial appearance of predictability, order, and design—is daunting. No one is running the show, so to speak—there is no one man behind the curtain. However, on balance, I have found this burgeoning perspective, particularly as applied to psychoanalysis and psychotherapy, remarkably clinically useful, if profoundly challenging to our usual and familiar ideas about development, cognition, affect, transference, countertransference, defense, trauma, and therapeutic action. In this chapter, I will share with you a perspective that is relatively new to our field, one variously and sometimes imprecisely described as nonlinear dynamic systems theory, catastrophe theory, chaos theory, complex adaptive systems theory, self-organized systems theory, and so forth. I prefer the designation *complexity theory* and, applied to psychoanalysis and psychotherapy, *psychoanalytic complexity*. Sometimes, however, it seems to be more of a perplexity theory than anything else.

The advent of applying complexity theory to an increasing number of disciplines, such as physics (Bak 1996; Prigogine 1996), molecular biology (Kauffman 1995), and information theory (Cover & Thomas 2006; and now even to the internet itself [Falk, 2012]), has encouraged many psychoanalytic theorists to follow suit. Kohut (1977) once remarked,

> If psychoanalysis is to remain the leading force in man's attempt to understand himself, and indeed if it wants to stay alive, it must respond with new insights when it is confronted with new data and thus with new tasks. (p. 268)

Psychoanalysts are beginning to grasp more clearly that "new data" unfold in surprising, sometimes unusual, and creative, nonlinear ways and that our theoretical perspectives must evolve along with them. This chapter—indeed, this entire book—reflects an additional step, one among many others, in this evolution. It addresses some of the basics of complexity theory and its broader implications for its inclusion in psychoanalytic thought. It also introduces some of the key attitudes emanating from psychoanalytic complexity, through which perspective we can consider clinical experience. This chapter does not aim to plunge you into the roiling and complicated waters of complexity theory as it is understood by molecular biologists or astrophysicists but instead stands as your invitation to consider more seriously the richness and utility of a multidisciplinary sensibility that has revolutionized our assumptions about the emergence and transformation of emotional life.

A complexity sensibility compellingly dissuades us from thinking of our world, including our experiential worlds, as containing disparate, unrelated parts (that is, if we are speaking *explanatorily*). At the same time, it underscores the idea that our experiential worlds often do not necessarily reflect, in a one-to-one, palpably-felt, correspondence fashion, the originary and contemporary sources of those worlds and the meanings we attribute to them. Whereas it posits a worldview fundamentally incompatible with presumptions we may have had about separateness of self and other, personal agency, free will, the individuality of personal minds, the solid, static nature of truth, emotional development as epigenetic and teleological, or the rule-based and design-based nature of the universe, a complexity sensibility nevertheless does not preclude the possibility of experiencing our selfhood and worldhood in a myriad of ways (that is, if we are speaking *phenomenologically*), including feeling radically separate, disengaged, estranged, or even nonexistent (Atwood 2011; Atwood, Orange, & Stolorow 2002). It is our attitude (our seventh attitude, that of making "distinctions between dimensions of discourse") about and the tension engendered by the ubiquitous discrepancy between these two levels of discourse—the *phenomenological* and the *explanatory*—that is heavily implicated in how we work clinically and in what ultimately proves to be mutative for our patients.[4]

Psychoanalytic complexity eschews the more radical relativism and deconstructionism found in postmodernism in favor of the more moderate *post-structuralism* of which Cilliers (1998) writes in his descriptions of complexity. Whereas the approaches of Derrida (1978) and Lyotard (1984), for instance, "acknowledge that it is not possible to tell a single and exclusive story about something that is really complex...the acknowledgement of complexity, however, certainly does not lead to the conclusion that anything goes" (Cilliers 1998, p. viii) or that everything is left up to social construction (Hacking 1999). Whereas emotional experience and meaning are not pictured as rule-driven, static, or hard-wired, they also are not envisioned as solely the result of interpretive activity and moment-by-moment construction by the analytic dyad. Instead, they are more profitably understood as emergent and patterned (or *soft-assembled*) through the cooperation of all the constituents of a relational system, in the past, present, and imagined future.

Psychoanalytic complexity offers us a richer paradigm with which to comprehend experiential worlds and the means by which we can convey a deeper respect for the complexity of human experiencing. This correlates with the first attitude addressed in the Introduction, that of an "unrelenting respect for the complexity of human experience and personal individuality." Second, it helps us understand more deeply the highly contextualized nature of emotional experience and the meanings we attribute to it—from which our second attitude is derived: "our relentless embeddedness in contexts from which we can never extricate ourselves." And third, it revolutionizes concepts such as human development, so-called psychopathology, and the process of change. In many respects, it is the logical extension of, and arguably the conceptual suprastructure for, psychoanalytic paradigms such as intersubjective systems theory (Stolorow et al. 2002), specificity theory (Bacal 2006), a variety of forms of relational theory (Aron 1996; Benjamin 2004; Davies 2004; Erhenberg 1992; Harris 2005; Hoffman 1998; Mitchell 2000; Pizer 1998; etc.), and other more radical contextualist perspectives—those that center on an appreciation of the role of context in understanding emotional experience and meaning, of relational engagement, and of the unpredictability and fluidity of emotional development. And not surprisingly, complexity theory directly opposes the philosophical and practical assumptions of many more traditional approaches to psychoanalysis and psychotherapy today. At its postmodern foundation lies a profound alteration in our more customary worldviews, one that invariably challenges our essential and perhaps more comfortable presumptions about truth, reality, the therapeutic relationship and, more broadly, the origins of emotional experience and emotional meaning. Psychoanalytic complexity is concerned with the emergence and patterning of emotional experience from the self-organization and cooperation of many parts, with the conditions necessary to produce adaptive change, and with the process of making meaning out of apparent randomness. Henri Atlan (1984), in the field of biophysics, comments that "randomness is a kind of order, if it can be made meaningful; the task of making meaning out of randomness is what self-organization is all about" (p. 110). And given the unpredictability inherent in this kind of randomness, we are bestowed, potentially, with a sense of hope that things might be different, that things might move in new and unimaginable directions, visions of which we may not yet be able to entertain. This speaks to our ninth attitude, that of *radical hope* (Lear 2007).

Theory Preference and the Incommensurability of Paradigms

Before addressing in detail several of the key facets of complexity theory, including its theoretical and clinical value, I briefly turn to the issue of theory preference and the problem of the incommensurability of paradigms (Kuhn 1962). When new ideas emerge on the horizon, they often, though not always, are couched in a deferential language. We witnessed this, for example, when Heinz Kohut began the psychoanalytic odyssey that would become self psychology. His seminal 1959 paper reflected not just the nascence of his revolutionary ideas about empathy, the primacy of lived experience, and the relationship between mode of observation and theory, but a deep respect for the work of Sigmund Freud and the accompanying qualifiers that Kohut and his colleagues were not exactly saying anything new. Subsequently he comments that he was pouring "new wine into old bottles" (1984, p. 114), redefining the meanings and implications of a variety of traditional concepts (e.g., defense and resistance) while often maintaining familiar psychoanalytic terminology. He would refer to the foundational compatibility of his perspective with that of his in-absentia mentor through invoking (and stretching the meaning of) the principle of complementarity (drawing from Bohr & Mottelson 1957)– meaning, for Kohut, that apparently disparate ideas, each emanating from its own necessarily discrepant perspective, can live together, can complement one another, in useful ways.

It was not until later in his career, the late 1970s, that Kohut (1977) more explicitly distanced himself from this view by asserting that his psychology of the self was more essential, more foundational, to the science of a pure psychology. Self psychology could account for a broader range of human experiencing and its developmental vicissitudes. Freudian theory became increasingly subsumed under this new perspective, or it was, in instances, opposed and rejected outright. The evolution of Kohut's reconceptualization of the Oedipal experience and its vicissitudes reflects a clear instance of this. This is all to highlight that the paradigm of complexity theory, as rigorously as we might desire its integration into and synthesis of more familiar ideas, stands as ultimately incommensurable with the more traditional perspectives that adhere to objectivist, positivistic assumptions about truth and reality (including psychic reality).

Kohut (1984) asserted that the "elimination of [psychoanalytic] terms, then, is crucial only when they contribute to the perpetuation of substantive conceptual errors" (p. 115). Psychoanalytic complexity does not necessarily argue for the elimination of psychoanalytic terminology, but rather, first and foremost, fosters an insistence on distinguishing between those that refer to lived, subjective *experience*, on one hand, and those that refer to theoretical *explanation*, on the other hand. Comprising one of the key attitudes derived from a complexity sensibility—our seventh attitude, as cited previously—this distinction obviates the invariable confusion that arises when the language of experience (phenomenology) and the language of theory (explanation) are conflated. As alluded to in the Introduction, the use of the term *self* provides a glaring example: Viewed through a psychoanalytic complexity theory lens, it denotes a dimension of experience and not a theoretical explanation for such an experience.

Psychoanalytic complexity does sport an unusual and impressive array of terms that are organized around theoretical explanation, not phenomenological description. A complex system, for instance, is not one in which one *feels* complex or chaotic or experiences the world as chaotic, though indeed we sometimes do. Rather, it is one that is loosely guided by principles of self-organization, nonlinearity, emergence, unpredictability, disequilibrium, and transformation. Psychoanalytic complexity does not describe or prescribe how we should feel but instead aims at understanding and explaining the emergence and vicissitudes of our experiences and the meanings we attribute to them. Thus, psychoanalytic complexity implicitly asks whether a specific term (e.g., selfobject or object representation) references a dimension of experience or a theoretical construct. It necessitates a greater specification of the meaning of the terms we do choose to use.

We can no longer think of our world, including our experiential world, as containing disparate, unrelated parts. Not only is the whole greater than the sum of its parts, as systems theorists are wont to say, but the parts—all the parts, without exception—are inextricably intertwined and ceaselessly embedded in a larger context. Psychoanalytic complexity reflects a worldview fundamentally incompatible with presumptions we may have had about separateness of self and other, the individuality of personal minds, the solid, static nature of truth, human emotional development as epigenetic and teleological, the rule-based and design-based nature of the universe, and so forth. It is rather unsettling to imagine how unstable, fluid, and unpredictable our existence and world really are despite appearances to the contrary.

Psychoanalytic Complexity and the Responsibility for Individual Experience

Complexity theory is relentlessly multidisciplinary and interdisciplinary. And no one invented it. One of its essential tenets, that of self-organization, is demonstrated in its very nature—how it developed and continues to be elaborated by highly innovative thinkers from a variety of disciplines such as mathematics (Poincaré & Guillaume 1900; Thom 1974), physics (Bak 1996), biology (Kauffman 1995; Waddington 1966), and meteorology (Lorenz 1993), to name just a few. In psychology, psychotherapy, and psychoanalysis, an increasing number of theorists are also finding complexity theory compelling and useful (Bacal & Herzog 2003; Beebe & Lachmann 2001; Bonn 2010; Charles 2002; Dubois 2003; Galatzer-Levy 1978; Ghent 2002; Harris 2005; Lichtenberg et al. 1992; Magid 2002; Marks-Tarlow 2011; Miller 1999; Moran 1991; Orange 2006; Palombo 1999; Pickles 2006; Piers 2005; Sander 2002; Sashin & Callahan 1990; Scharff 2000; Seligman 2005; Shane & Coburn 2002; Shane et al. 1997; Sperry 2011; Spruiell 1993; Steinberg 2006; Stolorow 1997; Sucharov 2002; Thelen 2005; Thelen & Smith 1994; Trop et al. 2002; VanDerHeide 2009; Varela et al. 1991; Weisel-Barth 2006); each seems to have his or her own take on it. And it is, to paraphrase Kauffman (1995), its own shortest description. It cannot be reduced down to something simpler than its surface appearance. And its surface appearance, to be sure, is not exactly simple, but it is certainly elegant and provocative.

And such is the case with experiential worlds; they are their own shortest description and are relentlessly irreducible—again, as reflected in our first attitude. They are not reducible to instinctual life, primitive defense mechanisms, relational configurations, self and object representations, or selfobject experiences. In fact, psychoanalytic complexity eschews the notion of intrapsychic representation (not to be confused with the action of consciously representing something via symbol), as well as the notion that emotional experience and meaning emanate from an inside, intrapsychic space concerned with the management of representations of an objective, external world. From an intersubjective systems perspective, Orange (2001) makes this vital distinction when she delineates the implications of Cartesian (and ultimately clinical) assumptions about the potential source of emotional experience as necessarily lying either inside of one's psyche, and hence subject to the distorting effects of one's subjectivity, or outside in the real world, the ultimate and true arbiter of truth and reality. She rightly states,

> this dichotomy is particularly dangerous in clinical work. Patients and analysts can become endlessly entangled in trying to determine where a particular reality lies, inside or outside, or where responsibility for a reaction, for a life pattern, or for some interpersonal disaster lies. (p. 291)

Instead of experiencing the *outside world* and then *internalizing* it, *representing* it, and arranging it in some manner for future adaptational use, sources of emotional experience are more usefully pictured as distributed throughout multiple relational systems. In that sense, in the explanatory sense, no one authors or owns his emotional experience. In the phenomenological sense—that is, how we actually experience things—we may very well feel that we are the authors and owners of our experiential worlds, though not necessarily always (see Atwood et al. 2002). To paraphrase Merleau-Ponty (1968), we can no longer say: This is mine and this is yours. This sensibility articulates with our eighth attitude, the "conundrum of personal situatedness, emotional responsibility, and potential (finite) freedom," which will be explored in more depth in the next chapter.

An advantage of psychoanalytic complexity, to extend Orange's (2001) perspective, is not just the purging of the inside-outside dichotomy in trying to account for the sources of emotional experience and their corresponding meanings but the elimination of the assumption that such experience and meanings can be attributed solely to one's history, one's current (*inside*) mental state, or one's immediate (*outside*) environment—yet another key attitude, our third one, derived from complexity theory, that "we are continually informed by our history, our current state, and our environment, and at no time can we definitively draw the lines between these sources of emotional experience." This false trifurcation, another clinical quagmire in which we are drawn into the hunt for the *true and real* sources of an individual's experience (i.e., Is it your history or your present, is it I or is it you, that accounts for your experience?) dissolves when we realize that at no moment can the source of an individual's experiential world be relegated to any one of the three and, furthermore, at no point can we ever draw an actual line (explanatorily speaking) between any of the three (i.e., this comes from your past, this comes from now, this comes from your environment, etc.). From a psychoanalytic complexity perspective, that would be akin to holding a single bird responsible for the flight trajectory of an entire flock (think of starlings over Scotland, not migrating ducks). And locating the lines of demarcation between each of the three would be tantamount to claiming to know simultaneously the position and momentum of a subatomic particle at a given moment in time. Working with this explanatory assumption is another instance of the powerful way in which attitudes impact the clinical setting.

Complex Adaptive Systems

Descriptively, complexity theory and the concept of complexity can be approached from a variety of angles, can be talked about in different ways. Indeed, each author who has written about it seems to highlight one or a few specific aspects of the idea in the course of applying it to psychotherapy and psychoanalysis, and there are many facets from which to choose. Some highlight the importance of initial conditions, some the property of self-organization, some focus on the concept of self-criticality (or a particular system's propensity toward hovering around the *tipping point*), some underscore the dynamism, fluidity, and unpredictability of a system, others the role of perturbation in altering the trajectory of a system, and still others the characteristic of emergence and the idea that nonlinear systems are not rule-driven or design-driven. There are many other descriptive aspects of the theory from which theorists draw useful metaphors if not direct explanations for understanding human experiencing and therapeutic action.

Briefly, let's look at the nature of a complex adaptive system and the concept of complexity itself. Complex systems comprise a large number of elements; this is a necessary but not sufficient condition of a complex system. The elements must interact in a dynamic fashion; this interaction does not have to be physical but often simply involves a transference of information from one component to another. Such interactions need to be rich, that is, each constituent in the system influences and is influenced by many others. Interactions are nonlinear; nonlinearity provides opportunities such that seemingly small causes may yield large results, just as apparently large causes or interventions may bring about relatively small results. Nonlinear interactions often have a short range. For example, one person has an immediate effect upon another when in close physical proximity, just as one neuron directly impacts its immediate neighbor only, but such interactions also have wide-ranging influences on components that are more distally located. Furthermore, elements in a complex system share the quality of recurrence, that is, the effect of any activity can feed back onto itself, sometimes directly, sometimes after a number of intervening stages—reflecting our fourth attitude, that of "autocatalysm and recurrence." Think of the process of speaking, or of painting: We adjust our words or brush strokes partly in response to our immediate experience of what was just spoken or of that last splash of color and texture on the canvas.

Complex systems are thought to be open, in the sense described by Thelen and Smith (1994); this means that they are capable of interacting with their environment and of taking in energy or information and making use of it in some way. They differentiate between two types of systems: closed and open. A closed system is one that has "run down to a state of entropic equilibrium" (p. 53) in which the system settles into a stable configuration. An open system, on the other hand, is "one that is stable yet far from thermodynamic equilibrium" (p. 53). This condition can be "maintained only by a continuous flow of free energy and matter into and out of the system" (p. 53). An open system is one that maintains

> equilibrium by drawing energy from a source of high-energy potential, doing work, and dissipating some of this energy, in turn, back to the environment…
> When sufficient energy is pumped into these systems, new, ordered structures may spontaneously appear that were not formerly apparent. (pp. 53–54)

It is this relentless intake and output of energy or information that maintains the system's relative state of disequilibrium, which is good for the system.

To speak of an open system as having an environment—that is, some type of *outside* arena in which the system is embedded and by which it is contextualized—necessarily implies a human observer choosing to draw a line between the two. When this is done—and it is only done for descriptive, thought-experiment purposes—it defines the system under study at that particular moment in time. Importantly, there are no standardized or codified lines of demarcation between systems and their environments, just as there are no clear and constant lines that can be drawn between the conscious and the unconscious (Stolorow & Atwood 1996). As Cilliers (1998) states, "[i]nstead of being a characteristic of the [complex] system itself, the scope of the system is usually determined by the purpose of the description of the system, and is thus often influenced by the position of the observer" (p. 4). This process of drawing lines for purposes of description or experimentation is referred to as *framing*. It is a way of defining specific potential systems as either a system, subsystem, or suprasystem; any element potentially can be considered a system in its own right, as can any system be understood as an element of a larger system, depending on the perspective, interests, and aims of the observer. For instance, we might speak of an individual person as a system in her own right, effectively defining the *environment* as everything else. Or, alternatively, we might choose to define the system as two individuals in close proximity, or as our entire world-bound sociocultural surround. It is up to you!

Complex, open systems, as mentioned earlier, function under conditions far from equilibrium. In the context of human life, equilibrium means demise. Moreover, a complex system has a history. Cilliers (1998) states, "Not only do they evolve through time, but their past is co-responsible for their present behaviour" (p. 4). This reveals the limitations of, for example, naïve constructivist or *here and now* perspectives in which psychological phenomena arising between two people are believed to be *constructed* in the moment, apart and somehow insulated from both individuals' relational histories.

Finally, the nature of a complex system is such that

> Each element in the system is ignorant of the behaviour of the system as a whole, it responds only to information that is available to it locally…If each element "knew" what was happening to the system as a whole, all of the complexity would have to be present in that element. (pp. 4–5)

For Cilliers (1998), the notion of each element "knowing" the status of the system as a whole constitutes either a "physical impossibility" or a leap to metaphysical descriptions.

And thus, we can begin to picture the revolutionary perspective offered by a complexity sensibility, how it reconceptualizes and recontextualizes human systems and their corresponding emotional worlds as profoundly open, fluid, dynamic, relatively unpredictable, relentlessly intertwined and interpenetrating, and without clear and pre-designed developmental programs or trajectories despite the outward appearance of design, order, and concreteness. As you can see by now, complexity theory, *at the very least*, serves to stimulate our minds and to challenge our otherwise familiar and comfortable assumptions about life and our world. Simply allowing yourself to contemplate this sensibility, in earnest, will necessarily alter who you are and what you do in the consultation room, not to mention in the balance of your life. In trying on an unusual theoretical perspective and in interacting in the consultation room, the analyst, to paraphrase Harris (2005), has to surrender to a process she cannot anticipate or predict if dyadic growth and emotional expansion are to become possibilities.

Complexity Itself

Given this view of complex adaptive systems, let us turn for a moment to the concept of complexity itself. Complexity has been defined in a variety of ways—two that are particularly interesting to me. Generally, it refers to a quality or characteristic of a gathering of constituents (e.g., biological cells, people, governments) that are related in some way (a system). It is assumed that such a system—an open system—is capable of: (1) absorbing and using an influx of energy, (2) behaving autocatalytically (self-generative and self-transformative), and (3) adapting to its environment to insure its survival and increased efficiency. There are many other characteristics of an open system (as discussed previously) but, given these essentials, the characteristic of complexity refers to the relative state of an open system such that it is more or less poised for and capable of change. This is what complexity theorists mean by *poised on the edge of chaos*, *self-criticality*, or *the tipping point*. Thus, complexity can be understood as the state of a system in which there is enough fluidity and randomness (or *chaos*) to allow for innovation, novelty, and change, on one hand, and in which there is enough order and apparent structure to allow for the sustaining and continuance of those changes that do occur, on the other hand. Understood in this way, a system can be said to be more complex the more centrally it is poised between the two ends of this spectrum: between order and chaos. A system that is less complex may have too much order, such that transformation is exceedingly slow and negligible, or it may exhibit too much randomness, such that change is too rapid, wild, and not sustainable. This is one way to talk about complexity.

Parenthetically, when we speak of people and complex systems in the context of psychoanalysis and psychotherapy, it is tempting to slide into thinking of an individual person as the complex system under investigation and as that which we aim to change. Yes, an individual person can be thought of as a complex system, but in the dynamic, contextualist world of human relationships, in which each individual is understood as a co-adaptive, mutually, and reciprocally organizing component of a larger complex adaptive system, it is essential that we think of the system under investigation as, at the least, the therapeutic dyad. Previously, I commented that "people alone do not change, systems change—and on multiple levels... apparent change is reiterated or distributed throughout all systems and their respective constituents, just as those constituents support or are responsible for those changes in the first place" (Coburn 2002, p. 671). This is only an initial, skeletal view, given that each individual belonging to a specific dyad has enumerable other relational connections to the past, present, and imagined future, and that these vast, interconnected experiential worlds, so many we can never know them, are responsible ultimately for the emergence of an individual's emotional experience. To extend Martin Buber's (1970) assertion that without the Thou, there is no I, we can say that without the greater relational system, there is no self.

The second definition of complexity, one to which I am especially drawn, refers to the property of incompressibility—a term originating in mathematics and information theory (see Chaitin 1990). Mathematicians and information theorists are interested in the degree to which a series of numbers, concepts, or processes can be reduced down or compressed for ease of representation. This can be accomplished with algorithms, using algorithmic compression (Taylor 2001), a series of logical statements (e.g., a computer program) that aim to describe (and perhaps give directions about) something in a shorter space than that which the thing occupies. A concrete example is the compression of ten numbers (say, ten instances of the number eight) into a convenient two number packet (i.e., the number eighty). This is easier than writing out the number eight ten times. Any degree of compressibility means no complexity, and vice versa. A string of ten randomly chosen prime numbers, however, is considered complex, or incompressible; it cannot be reduced down to an algorithmic statement (such as "multiply eight by ten") that is shorter than itself. In fact, if we think in terms of representing something, we would say that it (the string of ten randomly chosen prime numbers) is its own shortest description—*it can only be represented by itself*, by writing all of them out, one by one. And such is the case with human beings, their experiential worlds, and their corresponding evolving emotional meanings. Extending this definition of complexity (i.e., as incompressibility) to human experiencing and the meaning-making process has enormous implications for how we understand (and treat, in both senses of the term) people. In this light and given that we humans comprise complex systems, we can no longer understand our experiential worlds as compressible or representable, for instance, as drives or drive derivatives, a set of object relations, a configuration of neurobiological connections, a self structure with missing parts, or any other form of abbreviation of what is human. This articulates with our first attitude, "an unrelenting respect for the complexity of human experiencing and personal individuality." (The notion of diagnostically categorizing as a means of saying something substantial or meaningful about a person is anathema to psychoanalytic complexity.) The Freudian caricature of compressibility might be the reduction of an individual to the vicissitudes of his instinctual life or to the outcome of his Oedipal relations.

Traditionally, Western medicine, psychiatry, and psychology predicated the formulation of treatment approaches on arriving at a diagnostic conclusion. Once you knew what was wrong with your patient, treatment became clear. And sadly, all too often what was wrong with the patient was his peculiar and/or painful affect. To know a person was to superimpose a predesigned, previously codified, descriptive label over what otherwise was an infinitely complex, fluid, dynamic, relational being whose only accurate description can be understood as an emergent property and product of a larger dynamic system—one that is relentlessly unfolding, over time. The advantages inherent in tolerating not knowing, in remaining open to surprise and novelty, including the meaning of affect, were lost. There is nothing quite like the *Diagnostic and Statistical Manual* if you are looking for a convenient device to reduce the complexity and contextuality of experiencing and meaning-making down to two-dimensional caricatures of what is human. As Adam Phillips (1999) remarks, "fear of the unknown is cured through flight into the intelligible...The familiar, the unsurprising, restores our collusive sanity" (pp. 110–111). And what is to be diagnosed, reduced down, and rendered pathological—usually affect, mood, or behavior—is often also politically driven (Cushman 2011) and subject to the dictates of mainstream scientism. Indeed, the presumed medical and psychological authorities dictate what grants get funded, what is to be studied in laboratories, what gets taught, what is normal and, especially, what is human and what is not. It was this social, scientistic zeitgeist that, in part, inspired our postmodern movement as exemplified in the 1984 publishing of Lyotard's *The Postmodern Condition*. Not thinking contextually, as a means of protecting ourselves, perpetuates the narrowing of our personal affective freedom. Merleau-Ponty (1945/2002) was onto this when he said,

> I can miss being free only if I try to bypass my natural and social situation by refusing to take it up, in the first place, instead of assuming it in order to join up with the natural and human world. (pp. 529–530)

This is not to say, however, that as complex adaptive systems in our own right we (and the larger system of which we are all a part) are not capable of identifying, compressing, and storing important information about emotional experience (one of the hallmarks of a complex adaptive system, as distinct from an ocean wave or a weather pattern). Metaphorically, we can think of this type of compression of emotional knowledge as the implicit relational knowing to which D. N. Stern et al. (1998) and others refer, but keep in mind this type of knowing does not, of course, originate in a relational vacuum and likewise never emerges in one. Implicit relational knowing is always a product and property of a past, present, and imagined future relating with others (Fosshage 2005; Loewald 1972; D. N. Stern 2004) and can be understood as distributed throughout larger interpenetrating relational systems. In this sense, relational expectancies can usefully be understood more as relational potentialities that are completed and brought to life as products and properties of context. An aspect of the relational context (e.g., the analyst) here is not understood simply as a provocateur of another's isolated-mind template but as a system constituent that completes a potentiality. Contrary to traditional thought, you cannot hold one individual responsible for the sometimes-excruciating repetitiveness of relational expectancies and patterns that emerge in the context of a dyadic system.

Whereas experiential worlds are complex or incompressible and cannot be *reduced down* to something smaller and more easily understood, they can be envisioned as potentially represented—*witnessed* is a much better term (Orange 1995, 2011)—through the medium of the felt experience of the analytic therapy process itself, *as it unfolds, over time*. And the comprehension of witnessed, experiential worlds can emerge only through an open spirit of inquiry, our tenth attitude. In other words, we might say that experiential worlds are algorithmically *described*, over time, via their gradual unfolding and investigating in the context of the therapeutic relationship. They cannot be captured in one statement or one picture but must be understood as an unfolding, emerging, and relentlessly evolving human landscape that is insistently and continually shaped by one's history, current state, and environment—the lines between which, as I stated before, are forever indeterminate (our third attitude). In this sense, our lived lives, experienced, investigated, and understood over time, are their own shortest description. Therapeutic action, conveyed through our attitudes, in part arises from the explicit, articulated appreciation of this assumption. This is consonant with Orange's invocation of the concepts of fallibilism (1995) and the hermeneutics of trust (2011), which, for me, underscore the necessity of not only holding our theories lightly but also holding lightly the emergent and accrued truths and realities that coalesce within the analytic dyad from one day to the next or from one year to the next. This is what I think of as *epistemological ineptitude*, our sixth attitude: When it comes to claiming to know something, to reclining in the warm contentment of accrued knowledge, we frequently encounter, if we are honest with ourselves, our dubious modes of assessment and the painful limits and errors of our conclusions. Our experiential worlds are always changing as they are emerging and emerging as they are changing. As complexity theorists are wont to say, *the rules of the game change as a result of the play*.

Contextualist Paradigms, Complexity, and Emotional Life

The first decade of the work of Atwood and Stolorow—their intersubjective systems theory (beginning in 1977)—crystallized a cohesive and compelling alternative to traditional psychoanalytic theorizing (Atwood & Stolorow 1984). Among other themes, they emphasized the elucidation of the "nature, developmental origins, and functional significance of the psychological structures that prereflectively organize the patient's subjective experiences" (p. 46). At the same time, they argued that psychological phenomena arise out of "indissoluble psychological system[s]…system[s] that constitute the empirical domain of psychoanalytic inquiry" (p. 64). From a contemporary perspective, we might wonder, is it the patient's organization of experience that is grasped and articulated, or is it *systemically derived* configurations of experience that are the subject matter of investigation? By the next decade, particularly in Stolorow's 1997 essay on dynamic, dyadic systems, referred to in the Preface, and in Orange, Atwood, and Stolorow's book, *Working Intersubjectively* (1997), they more robustly conceptualized the psychoanalytic investigation of psychological phenomena from the standpoint of a more radical contextualism in which the subject matter of psychoanalysis is taken to be systemically derived patterns of experience that often appear to manifest experientially on the local level of the individual. Alternatively stated, Orange et al. observed that the "intersubjective viewpoint does not eliminate psychoanalysis' traditional focus on the intrapsychic [the local level]. Rather, it contextualizes the intrapsychic" (p. 67).

Trop et al. (2000, 2002) then drew on the work of Thelen and Smith to question the use of structuralism in intersubjective systems theory. In particular, they critiqued the language embedded in assumptions of invariant structures and principles. They alternatively proposed the use of the terms *perceived experiential patterns* and *attractor states* in place of *structures of subjectivity* and *organizing principles*, respectively. Such a proposed modification in language advanced us toward a more robust nonlinear, open systems sensibility to an even more experience-near perspective of psychological phenomena. For me, however, terms such as *attractor state* have an experience-distant flavor, whereas a phrase such as *perceived experiential patterns* underscores the experience-near ambience frequently associated with intersubjective systems theory. Of course, this latter phrase invites the question, perceived by whom? This necessarily prompts us to ask how, exactly, contours of experience are explored and how patient and analyst collaboratively arrive at agreed-on visions of experience and meaning.[5]

Other theorists also extend a nonlinear, open-systems perspective to psychoanalysis. Connectionism, parallel distributed processing, and the concept of empathic network, as discussed by Arnetoli (1999), represent an exciting elaboration of systems thinking in the dyadic, psychoanalytic context. The work of Sucharov (1994, 2002), including his concept of *empathic contact*, similarly extends the anti-Cartesian, anti-representational spirit of systems theory. Essentially, these perspectives understand psychological phenomena in any form (e.g., a dream, an emotional experience) as distributed across a network of which each individual is a part. Psychological phenomena, then, are conceptualized as potentially emergent at the local level (e.g., in the experiential domain, perhaps, but not necessarily of one person only) and as dyadically or systems-generated emotional events as well. Depending on the resolution of the *frame*, psychological phenomena, for instance, can be conceptualized as distributed across the neural network (as opposed to located within a specific neuron or set of neurons) of a singular brain, across multiple neural networks (as opposed to located within a singular brain), or across multiple systems of neural networks (as opposed to one dyadic system or intersubjective field). In the spirit of complexity theory, these phenomena are understood as arising out of the nonlinear, self-organizing interactions between the system's history, current state, and environment.

Arnetoli (1999) states that psychological phenomena or "entities are localistic and subjective but they are also systemic and parallel-distributed" (p. 24). Likewise, Sucharov (2002) posits that the "interpenetration of experience in the analytic encounter dislodges experience from the tidy compartment of intrapsychic space and spreads it throughout the relational field" (p. 687). Hence, psychological phenomena are of *ambiguous ownership*, and are relentlessly, spontaneously emergent. From a relational perspective, Ringstrom (2001) provides a striking illustration of spontaneous, emergent experience in the form of improvisational relating, in which the therapist exercises her latitude for spontaneous, self-expression without the encumbrances of immediate reflection. Hoffman (1998) also addresses the potential and therapeutically necessary spontaneous relating so central to therapeutic action in his elaboration of his invitation to the analyst to be open to stepping outside the ritualistic and bounded forms of psychoanalytic practice, effectively "throwing away the book" (1994, p. 194). Though not exactly coextensive, Knoblauch's (2000) concept of *action time*, in contrast to *listening time*, provides an elegant instance of appreciating ambiguously owned and emergent affective life between people:

> The experience of action time between two people feeling, thinking, speaking together is different from that of listening time, especially in psychoanalysis. Psychoanalysis is the creation of an imaginative place, a way of attending and affecting, where time and space absorb, stretch, and contract in an interwash... In action time, emotions are continuously evaporating, condensing, or absorbing into each other. (p. 2)

I believe this type of experiencing and relating especially dramatizes sudden, systemically derived, emergent emotional life evidenced on the *local level* of the therapist's and patient's true-self functioning.

In her groundbreaking work on the soft-assembly of gender and the developmental applications of nonlinear dynamic systems theory, Harris (2005) emphasizes the high degree of context-sensitivity and context-dependency in language development and the formation of the sense of gender. She states that "[i]ndividuality arises within a matrix of significant others and relational experiences" (p. 89) and is always a product and property of larger sociocultural systems.[6] The development of individuality, for instance, "is not a matter of stepping up a ladder but moving through a kaleidoscope, weaving and being woven into a web of meaning and narration" (p. 93). Similarly, Piers (2000) applies a complexity perspective to reconceptualizing how we understand *character*. "In health," he states, "character could be conceived of as a system which remains poised in a chaotic region [a high degree of complexity], able to respond and remain sensitive to internal fluctuations and external perturbations" (p. 26). In this light, individual character, however fixed it may appear, is always potentially informed by the complex human systems that support it, just as those systems are in turn influenced by the character formation to which they are giving rise (Piers

2005). Seligman (2005) has also contributed substantially to reconceptualizing the notion of the individual through a complexity theory lens. In this light, psychoanalysis, including the therapeutic process, *is a dyadic and dynamic system* in its own right, highly interactive and self-organizing; no one person is running the show.

Thus, the subject matter of psychoanalytic investigation might be reconceived to include not only the lived, subjective experience of the patient but the systemic interactions, including the development and use of language and other forms of symbolization (Harris 2005), that constitute the shape and form of that experience and that imbue it with a sense of aliveness, spontaneity, expansiveness, and meaning (our fifth attitude—that of "valuing the 'feeling' of complexity, in the phenomenological sense"). And here is an important distinction; we may more usefully think of these modes of patterning of experience, or experiential contours,[7] not as operating in the background, not as giving rise to personal experience itself, but rather as the actual, unique, emergent experience at hand. In other words, it is conceptually useful to resist dichotomizing experiential patterns or themes and the experiences themselves. Rather than conceiving of experience and context as being analogous to a river and its riverbed, in which the water and the contours by which it is shaped are two, extricable entities, emotional experience and its specific contours or character are inseparable; they are one and the same. To borrow Orange et al.'s (1997) use of medieval philosophical distinctions, differentiating between experiential contours and the experiences themselves might be understood as "distinctions of reason…entities without real plurality" (p. 70), whereas the water and riverbed analogy illustrates "real distinctions… entities thought to be actually divisible" (p. 70). Experiential contours do not reside either within the unconscious of the patient or within that of the analyst but, rather, they lie at the interface of a myriad of self-organizing components of which the patient and the analyst represent a few.

This applies to the notion of the self as well, whether pictured as unitary or as multiple. Piers (2005) usefully addresses this complexity-oriented conceptualization of the self:

> From my reading of literature on multiplicity of selves, however, it is not clear whether those who speak of multiplicity are suggesting that the multiple versions of the self lie dormant until activated by the relational context, or whether the immediate relational context draws aspects of subjective experience together in previously unanticipated ways to form internally generated, externally informed, and context-specific selves. The latter would be closer to the meaning intended in complexity theory. (p. 249)

Why is this distinction so important? As germane to understanding emotional life as the concept of organizing principles is, making this distinction helps subvert our natural human proclivity to reduce an individual's emotional world down to the (often unconscious) organizing principles thought to reside *inside* the individual—

potentially another form of isolated mind thinking, in which we may hold, perhaps unintentionally, the individual responsible for his emotional convictions. That is not to say that relational potentialities—non-conscious, implicit, potential ways of experiencing and being with others—are not always virtually present somewhere. It *is* to assert, however, that when experiential contours based on those potentialities do emerge, the principles and the experiences that emanate from them are inseparable and always form from within a larger relational context (such as a therapeutic relationship, group of people, or the broader sociocultural surround).

What, then, is an additional way of understanding the rises and contours of lived, subjective experience? One promising answer lies in understanding the self-organizing capacity/activity of a multitude of complex, interpenetrating systems and their various constituents. These constituents, in and of themselves, are not conceptualized as *containing* any experiences, just as individual neurons are no longer thought of as containing specific memories (Edelman 1992). Similarly, whereas we tend to think of a person as *containing* experience (the Cartesian isolated-mind model)—after all, who is it that does the experiencing?—we also now understand that there would be no experience without the interaction of interpenetrating systems of which that person, along with many others, is a member. A standard criticism of this perspective manifests in the question, "But what about the role of fantasy in one's intrapsychic life, the fact that a person can have an 'individual' experience, for example, while skiing down a mountain, entirely alone?" This line of inquiry unsuccessfully attempts to bypass our knowledge that individuals develop, from the moment of conception, in a particularized system that is highly contextualized and quintessentially relational and that one's physical aloneness at a given point in time does not negate one's relational, systemic history and one's continued embeddedness in a specific world context (important attributes of all complex systems). Even the experience of a sensory deprivation tank is highly contextualized and does not place one suddenly into the realm of the Cartesian isolated mind, even though the experience very well may be one of isolation and aloneness. Psychological phenomena originate from, are sustained by, and are modified in response to living, intersubjective systems. In any situation, individuals are continually affected by interpenetrating intersubjective systems, past and present, and are always shaped and sustained by the current surround, human and nonhuman alike. To think otherwise decontextualizes the person, effectively separating her from the systems in which she is embedded. This reduces the person from the status of a constituent of a complex system to that of being simply a member of a complicated one in which the whole can be reduced to the sum of its parts. In complex systems, such a view is untenable.

Experience, then, takes form and continues to transform dynamically out of multiple, interpenetrating systems. Whereas we understand emotional experience to be systemically derived, it is never informed entirely by the vicissitudes of one system alone, no more than a single neuron in one's brain determines the distribution and character of neural firing throughout a neurological network (Edelman 1992). Whereas seemingly evolving *in* the context of a psychoanalytic relationship, for example, during an analytic hour, emotional experience necessarily arises at any given moment from within multiple contexts simultaneously, since we do not actually *move* from one system to another as we might walk from one room to the next. Relational enactments between patient and therapist, for instance, when understood as repetitive only of the patient's archaic relationship patterns, denudes the patient-therapist relationship of its unique, dynamic, nonlinear, context-sensitive character. Systems—although they seem at moments to recede into the background—never die, and hence, we continue to be *of* all of them, as a living constituent, on an ongoing basis.[8] This is what is meant by the interpenetration of multiple, complex systems. Furthermore, systems are not solely interpenetrating, but they are also interactive, as must be evident by now, such that one or more systems help to shape and inform the dynamics of others, and vice versa. Here, using the process of framing, we may ask: Is it useful to think in terms of certain systems that feel more experientially central, salient, and relevant to the participants than others? This question is germane to the analytic dyad's exploration of emotional experience and meaning, to how the participants arrive at and organize their conclusions about the patient's subjective world from one moment to the next.

And Now for Something Really Strange: Bohm's World and the Coalescence of Experience

Bohm's (1980) idea of wholeness and the implicate order provides us with another useful metaphor for certain psychological phenomena, particularly unformulated perceptions, that appear to lie dormant and embedded within an undifferentiated medium of potential. Bohm's perspective offers a creative complement to and enhancement of complexity theory, particularly as it pertains to the concept of unformulated (D. B. Stern 1997) and dysformulated (Stolorow, Orange, & Atwood 2001b) experience in human relating. An important facet of analytic exploration lies not just in the illumination of an individual's contours of experience but in an acknowledgment that these contours exist in varying degrees of formulation and clarity, or consciousness. Bohm's work offers a model that usefully incorporates these less clear dimensions of experience and meaningfully supplements a complexity perspective.

Godwin (1991) describes the essence of Bohm's thinking as it pertains to the concepts of *the implicate*, *the explicate*, and *wholeness*. Here he suggests new ways of conceptualizing the evolution of personal experience from a systems perspective. Godwin states:

> Perhaps the most significant discovery of quantum physics is the disclosure of a fundamental realm of unbroken wholeness underlying our perceived world of apparent separateness and fragmentation. Instead of analyzing the universe

into parts and then trying additively to make a "whole" out of how they interact, Bohm therefore begins with this notion of an underlying, undivided wholeness, and then attempts to show how amidst this wholeness there may exist the "relatively enduring subtotalities" available to our senses and scientific instruments. Language becomes problematic at this point, because the deeply dualistic bias in its subject-verb-object structure presupposes a universe of individual parts in external relationship to one another. This outward order described by conventional language is what Bohm refers to as the "explicate," or "unfolded" order [think of our ongoing, conscious experience]. But underlying this explicate order is the vast multidimensional sea of quantum potential which forms the constantly unfolding common ground of the manifest universe. This prior and fundamental order of the universe Bohm calls the "implicate" (or enfolded) order. This order exists as "undivided flowing movement without borders" (Bohm 1980, p. 172), *and what may appear stable to our senses is simply a rapidly iterating succession of similar forms.* (p. 628, my italics)

Note here, among other important ideas, the high degree of compatibility between Bohm's views and the fluidity, dynamism, and absence of hard structure implicit in complexity theory. Bohm's model also allows for analogies to the parallel distributed processing and empathic contact concepts described by Arnetoli (1999) and Sucharov (1994, 2002), respectively. Whereas much of Bohm's theorizing intends on elaborating a rather different, postmodern view of physics and the workings of the universe, he himself recognizes the implications of his work for the study of consciousness. He states that the "general tenor of the implicate order implies that what happens in our own consciousness and what happens in nature are not fundamentally different in form. Therefore thought and matter have a great similarity of order" (Bohm 1980, p. 100, as cited in Godwin 1991, p. 630).

Translocating Bohm's (1980) evocative ideas and terminology into the psychoanalytic context, we can say that the explicate order comprises those emotional experiences that are felt to contain meaning and on which the analytic participants remain focused from one moment to the next: that is, the actual, systemically derived contours of emotional experience. In contrast, the implicate order suggests an infinite array of perceptions and potential perceptions that are not currently in focus in the sense of their containing emotional interest and meaning. The utility of this perspective is that experience that remains *dormant* or unformulated can usefully be understood as residing in a "vast multidimensional sea of [psychological] potential," rather than as entirely nonexistent or as in an objectified, concrete, unconscious state of repression in the Freudian sense. Bohm's concept of the implicate offers a powerful metaphor for conceptualizing the interpenetration of all systems as a whole, just as his idea of the explicate helps us to grasp the highly particularized nature of personal lived experience from one moment to the next.

And so, by now, we can sense that things are perhaps a bit more, well, complex than we might have previously imagined. Also, we may now see and perhaps appreciate more deeply the power and robustness of using this sensibility as an explanatory framework. To repeat an oft-quoted question that perpetually echoes throughout the halls of institutes and conference hotels, "But what do I *do* with this, clinically?" With this overview of complex systems, complexity, and our alternate ways of conceptualizing the emergence of emotional experience, let us turn to exploring in the next chapter a variety of attitudes that emanate from psychoanalytic complexity and the impact they have on the clinical surround.

Notes

1 From Jonathan Spence (1985) *The Memory Palace Of Matteo Ricci*. New York: Penguin, p. 267. Copyright © 1983, 1984 by the Jonathan D. Spence Children's Trust. Used by permission of Viking Penguin, a division of Penguin Group (USA) Inc.

2 Maurice Merleau-Ponty (1968) *The Visible and the Invisible*, trans. Alphonso Lingis. Evanston, IL: Northwestern University Press, p. 3. English translation copyright ©1968 by Northwestern University Press. All rights reserved.

3 From Jack Drescher's interview with Stephen Mitchell, 1994 in *The White Society Voice*. New York: William Alanson White Institute and the William Alanson White Psychoanalytic Society. Reprinted with permission, © 1994, The William Alanson White Psychoanalytic Society and © 2013, Contemporary Psychoanalysis (Journal of the William Alanson White Institute and the William Alanson White Psychoanalytic Society). All Rights Reserved.

4 A third potential dimension of discourse, discussed later, is referred to as *interpretive understanding* and pertains to unconscious organizing themes.

5 I have addressed this issue elsewhere in detail (Coburn 2001a).

6 As regards the development of the sense of individuality, Frie and I examined and explored this topic in depth in *Persons In Context: The Challenge of Individuality in Theory and Practice* (2011).

7 The use of this term was stimulated by Stolorow, Orange, and Atwood (2001b).

8 This crucial distinction involving the use of the term *of* was put forth and elaborated by Trop, Burke, and Trop (2000).

Chapter 5

Attitudes at Play

You may find yourself living in a shotgun shack
You may find yourself in another part of the world
You may find yourself behind the wheel of a large automobile
You may find yourself in a beautiful house with a beautiful wife
You may ask yourself, well, how did I get here?
                                    —'Once in a Lifetime,' Talking Heads[1]

...in so far as I am the instrument of possibilities which are not my possibilities...
I am *in* danger.
                                    —Jean Paul Sartre[2]

Any theoretical perspective has at its roots an array of presumptions and attitudes grounded in a specific worldview. As was argued in Chapter 2, there are no presuppositionless vantage points; one necessarily must stand *somewhere*. Now with an overview of complexity and complex systems in mind, let us turn to some of the key attitudes found in this rich and multifaceted sensibility and consider their potential impact on the clinical surround. Naturally we will not witness all ten of these attitudes operative in the foreground in every complexity-informed clinical instance or relationship, nor should we; some may be more manifest in some situations than in others. And most certainly, our patients may not necessarily experience our complexity-informed attitudes in the way we may experience them; intersubjective disjunctions are ubiquitous and must always be considered and investigated in our clinical work. Moreover, our language in real-time interactions will not—certainly should not—always reflect an overt complexity sensibility. Often, we speak with conviction when we feel we do know something. Often, we speak to patients in words that reflect a concrete understanding of what appears to be their individual personalities, as if they are stand-alone phenomena and not relevant to context. In day-to-day, clinical language, anything goes, really. Indeed, every therapeutic dyad naturally creates its own idiosyncratic language-games (Wittgenstein 1953/2001). As is often said, what is spoken or done entirely depends on context and does not necessarily always sound overtly like contextualizing an individual's experiential world. Through our underlying clinical attitudes, however, we hope to convey an ongoing openness to newer, updated points of view about our presumptions and convictions. In the upcoming clinical example, all ten attitudes may not be immediately evident, though we may continue to look for them. Once having written this clinical story, I considered, as a thought experiment, in what way my own complexity-informed attitudes may have played a role in helping shape what happened. This chapter emerged as the result of my reflections on those attitudes, some of which are found in our list of ten attitudes and which I felt helped contribute to the developmental dimensions of my work with Clarice. I will turn to these issues shortly.

As referenced in the Introduction, our ten attitudes include, but are not limited to, acknowledging and valuing the following presumptions:

1 An unrelenting respect for the complexity of human experiencing and personal individuality

Emotional experience and its corresponding meanings can no longer be understood as solely the result of neuronal firing encased in a hardened shell or simply the unfolding of a preexisting or predesigned genetic pattern. In a world of complex systems, no one set of components of a system, or what we might think of as predesign, can be held responsible for what emerges next. Being quintessentially contextualized beings, relentlessly shaping and being shaped by a highly specific and dynamic world, we humans are profoundly irreducible and are perpetually in transition from one state to the next. We certainly cannot be reduced to a diagnostic category if we are to maintain our sense of uniqueness, individuality, humanness, and passion for the unexpected. This includes a sense of compassion (Orange 2006) toward the peculiarities and specificity (Bacal 2011) of each of our emotional worlds and an appreciation for how an individual is uniquely situated in the world from one moment to the next. This is a valuable expansion of our continuing attempts to leave behind the more traditional veridicality-distortion dichotomy (Brenner 1979; Gill 1984) as we listen to an individual's narrative (is this *transference* or is this *real*? [Adler 1980]). This also highlights and cautions us about our natural propensity to slide into truth and reality assessments at the expense of relentlessly attending to emotional meaning—a sine qua non of the analytic endeavor.

2 Our relentless embeddedness in contexts from which we can never extricate ourselves

A spirit of unremitting contextualism, found in several paradigms such as intersubjective systems theory (Stolorow 1997), is foundational to a psychoanalytic complexity sensibility. This attitude also presumes individual, inescapable, context-embedded prejudices (Gadamer 1991) and the impossibility of even temporary disembeddedness from such personal situatedness. There are no *time-outs* from embodying our necessarily delimited experiential horizons, or metaphysical extrications from the human systems we are attempting to comprehend (von Foerster 1981). I have frequently been asked in conversations about relationality and contextuality whether there might be exceptional moments in which our experiential worlds might somehow be rendered apart and separate from our intersubjective fields or complex systems. As the question was posed in Chapter 4, what about when you are skiing down a mountain, entirely alone, with absolutely no one in sight? First, with a few exceptions, that might not be such a great idea—it's always wise to ski with a buddy. To the point: However *alone* one might be, one couldn't even be skiing, let alone thinking or experiencing, were it not for the unrelenting relational, sociocultural, and physical surrounds that gave one life, supports one's life, and propelled one to the top of the mountain in the first place. We perpetually live, and quite literally breathe, in the systemic contexts without which we would never have existed. I have also been asked, what is *context*, by the way? In short, *we* are context.

I am reminded of Henry James' (1881) *The Portrait of A Lady*, in which the protagonist speaks to how intensely contextualized we beings are:[3]

> When you've lived as long as I you'll see that every human being has his shell and that you must take the shell into account. By the shell I mean the whole envelope of circumstances. There's no such thing as an isolated man or woman; we're each of us made up of some cluster of appurtenances. (p. 287)

3 We are continually informed by our history, our current state, and our environment, and the lines between these sources of our experience remain forever indeterminate

This assumption is essential to understanding the emergence of emotional life and the meanings we attribute to it. An aspect of our existence as quintessentially contextualized beings is that we have a history that impels and propels us, we have a present in which our lives unfold in our perpetually moving toward what will be our next present, and we have an environment that we act upon just as it acts upon us (see Heidegger's [1927] concept of *ecstatic temporality*). Here, environment can be defined in any way you wish—it is up to you. It is anything that you consider outside of or other than what you think of as your self from one moment to the next, and, of course, whatever that may be will change and fluctuate as time passes. What is clinically crucial is that this attitude assumes that we can never relegate a facet of a person's experiential world (e.g., an emotional conviction or an affect state) solely to his history, to his current state of mind, or to his environment, and that the lines of demarcation between them are dynamic and fluid. These multiple sources of our experiential worlds and the meanings we attribute to them are always active. And just as we are continually informed by our history, our current state of mind, and our current environment, we are likewise perpetually shaped by our past, our present, and our imagined future (Loewald 1972; D. N. Stern 2004). And at no time can the lines be clearly delineated among these essential sources of our experiential worlds as well.

4 Autocatalysm and recurrence

This attitude, that the very components of a system produce their own agent of change and that what emerges from within a given system can feed back on itself, altering its previous state, profoundly alters how we traditionally had conceptualized therapeutic action: that is, the notion that one person acting on or toward another is what effects change. In this more contemporary light, it allows for the likelihood that the agent of change emerges as a product and property of the relational system itself. Valuing the concept of autocatalysm includes assuming the advantage of courting surprise and of accepting the inevitability of being startled in the midst of our clinical work. This attitude acknowledges that novelty can emerge at any moment, and it is left to us to determine the usefulness and meaning of what does emerge. And further, what might emerge at any moment is understood as a product and property of the highly contextualized, dialogic exchange in analysis—what Winnicott (1971) so beautifully underscored in his conceptualization of play between people. What does emerge is always a property and product of the larger system of which each of us is a part.

What causes a fish to wake up one morning, grow legs, and walk out of the ocean? She certainly wasn't designed to behave that way. Instead, as with any biological organism, she held in her organic structure a variety of design potentialities—potentialities with constraints—which, history and environment depending, may or may not be unleashed and realized. Human consciousness and our capacity for reflection, presumably distinguishing us from all other life forms on earth, are similarly emergent properties not previously designed or *meant to be*. Instead, legs, as well as consciousness, suddenly (that is, in geologic time) emerged because something in the context—innumerable variables and system components in interaction with each other—produced something new, which, in turn, acted upon these organisms, effectively inviting them to perform differently. And who could resist an invitation like that? Once consciousness or legs get going, their own actions in and on the world necessarily feed back on themselves (recurrence), which, in turn, invites more change, more transformation; more potentialities are realized. Next thing we know, we have lizards and iPhones.

5 Emergence, nonlinearity, and valuing the "feeling" of complexity in the phenomenological sense

This refers to the process of bringing emotional relating and themes to life and to learning to sense and recognize its emergence. In complexity theory, the word *complexity*, as addressed in Chapter 4, has very specific and sometimes discrepant meanings (e.g., the state of an open system and the characteristic of it not being reducible or compressible to something smaller or simpler). And normally it is not used to describe an experience (the *phenomenological*). Instead, it is usually meant to describe a particular state (the realm of the *explanatory*) of a system, one poised for imminent change. However, when this term is employed in the phenomenological sense—pertaining to lived subjective experience—it refers to the *feel* of a relational system, one that actually feels in flux and poised for change in which something unusual is emerging: a new and exciting way of relating. This renders an attitude that invites the therapeutic dyad to sense and feel when their system is in flux and ready to change in— ideally—positive directions. These moments can be marked, addressed, and commented on. A dyad can learn to sense when their system is in flux and headed in unpredictable directions, which is good, as opposed to living in the quagmire of what feels like the repetitive, the usual, the familiar, and perhaps the comfortable. The nonlinearity aspect of this attitude refers to the by-now familiar idea that seemingly small events may lead to large and meaningful outcomes—what euphemistically has been referred to as the *butterfly effect* (Lorenz 1963). This articulates with the emphasis in complexity theory on the role of initial conditions, first reflected in the work of Henri Poincaré (Poincaré & Guillaume 1900).

To more palpably grasp the *experience* of complexity—that is, the feel of a complex system at work and poised at the point of self-criticality, ready for change—consider your foot while driving in heavy traffic (think Los Angeles or perhaps Rome). You are perpetually alternating between accelerator and brake, back and forth, accelerator and brake. You are hardly aware of it. Cars in front of you, unpredictable as always, are starting and stopping, slowing and speeding up. You and your foot are continually managing split-second decisions about which pedal to engage. And now think of this: Occasionally you may find your foot, seemingly involuntarily (and procedurally [D. N. Stern et al. 1998]), rapidly moving back and forth between accelerator and brake pedal, as if it doesn't yet know where to land. I am speaking about the hovering, slight micro-movements of your foot that is situated *between* the two pedals. This rapid oscillation, until your seemingly fickle foot commits to a decision in the face of increased predictability, provides the feel of a high degree of complexity in which things are in flux and poised for the next change in one direction or another. Emotional worlds and our meaning-making processes often operate in a similar fashion. Sometimes, specific aspects of our experiential worlds—for instance, rapid meaning-making in the face of unfamiliar stimuli—oscillate between two or more ways of perceiving something: My analyst is caring about me, my analyst is judging me, my analyst is indifferent to me. When the force of oscillation is at its peak, poised for change and for redirection into something clear and definitive, self and world are in flux. These are moments of complexity (Taylor 2001) toward which we strive.

6 Embracing epistemological ineptitude

As alluded to previously, this attitude conveys a deep respect for the limits of our knowledge and aims to keep us alert to experiences of resolution, equilibrium, complacency, and generally settling into the false presumption that we have things pretty much figured out and do not have much more to learn (see Orange 2003a, and *perspectival realism* and *fallibilism*). Our attitude of epistemological ineptitude, akin to Orange's (1995) concept of fallibilism, affords us a sense of emotional conviction about our arrived-at truths but simultaneously invites us to hold such truths lightly, leaving room for a change in or expansion of those truths in the next moment, the next day, or the next year. This attitude articulates with that of the concept of incompressibility (the second way of defining complexity). Human experiencing and meaning-making are irreducible or incompressible and can be witnessed only as a function of time as one's experiential world unfolds, over time. Analytic exploration and meaning-making are not a process of unpacking an individual's intrapsychic or *internal* world with the aim at arriving at static truth, nor are they a process of negating the presence of individual minds and personal idiosyncrasy, presumably shaping the malleable mind of the patient with the analyst's interpretive activity alone. What is emerging is changing, and the change process then informs what emerges next. In this light, we would do well to attempt to hold our arrived-at truths and emotional convictions lightly.

Arriving at conclusions and then comfortably and complacently sitting on them, providing us with the illusion of being situated on firm and recognizable ground, are the bane of psychoanalysis and psychotherapy, but frequently we can't help it. Keats (1899) criticized this ubiquitous human trait when he spoke of his oft-referenced concept, *negative capability*. In an 1817 letter to his brothers, Keats alludes to this human proclivity to engage in the "irritable reaching after fact and reason" (1899, p. 277). *Negative capability* refers to the characteristic of being "capable of being in uncertainties, mysteries, doubts" (1899, p. 277).[4] Bion (1970) proffered a potential corrective to our irritable reaching in his recommendations to suspend "memory and desire" (p. 43) and to enter each clinical hour as if there were an entirely new individual sitting in front of you, each time. Whereas this may be practically unrealistic, and perhaps, if achievable, not the best idea, the spirit of this practice articulates well with our wish always to be open to new data, to novel experience, and to casting our assumptions aside in favor of thinking creatively. Novelty and surprise are always potentially imminent.

7 Distinctions between dimensions of discourse—the phenomenological and the explanatory/metaphysical

This attitude underscores the importance of not conflating two very distinct levels of discourse—one pertaining to lived, subjective experience and the other to the explanatory frameworks we might invoke to understand and describe such experience. One result of conflating the two is the reification of dimensions of experience, essentially reducing them down to constructs that then take on a concrete life of their own and thus inform one's worldview. As we explored in Chapter 4, a striking characteristic of complex systems, especially when applied to the domain of human experiencing, is the ubiquitous discrepancy between how systems work and how systems feel. That is, individual emotional life is pictured here as an emergent property of larger, interpenetrating relational systems, of which each of us is a constituent, and not as the product of one specific component or person. Thus, whereas I may experience my emotional world as mine, it is understood explanatorily as derivative of a larger relational network. A dramatic implication of this metaphysical assumption is that, despite however much we may feel a sense of ownership and/or authorship of our own emotional lives, it is the systemic context that gives rise to and defines such life. On the one hand, then, we consequently and ultimately cannot claim complete ownership or authorship of our emotional lives, but instead we are often left with a sense of having been propelled into a specific emotional and life situation. This reflects an instance in which the *phenomenological* directly reflects the *explanatory*. Heidegger (1927) referred to such situatedness as *Befindlichkeit* or *how-one-finds-oneself-ness* (see also Stolorow 2007, p. 2). And yet, on the other hand, despite the unremitting contextuality of one's personal situatedness, one must take what one has been given and claim it to be one's own or most certainly suffer the consequences of an attenuated existence or outright disavowal, phenomenologically speaking. As we shall see, this argument is fleshed out in our next outline point—our eighth attitude.

A closer examination of this distinction between dimensions of discourse reveals the usefulness of refining it somewhat, which includes the addition of a third dimension not previously addressed—the realm of *interpretive understanding*. Let us revisit these dimensions, including the addition of this third level of discourse, in turn.[5] Beginning with the first, phenomenological description refers to a realm of discourse grounded in felt experience that can variously range across a wide spectrum of relative states of formulation. Whereas this range of states can extend to relatively vague, unformulated though nevertheless potentially accessible states of mind and mood (D. B. Stern 1997), it primarily includes those emotional experiences that are conscious and articulable and, thus, those that can be reflected on. In this realm of discourse, speaking of *the self* would refer to one's *experience* of oneself, or selfhood—anxious, sad, calm, perplexed, disoriented, centered, and so forth. And it can refer to the experience of having parts or aspects of oneself from one moment or one physical context to the next, which is a prerequisite for the experience of personal conflict. In this language, referring to *this part of me* or *that part of me* acknowledges aspects of our felt experiential world residing in various degrees of accessibility and/or disavowal and not the presumption of the presence of any objectified psychic parts that are sometimes presumed to be dormant and sometimes not (i.e., something akin to the Freudian dynamic unconscious).

The second level of discourse, *interpretive understanding*, pertains to organizing principles that variously and context-dependently shape an individual's experiential world, including the coalescence of emotional meaning that gets associated with aspects of that experiential world. Like phenomenological description, this realm is both process- and content-organized, in that emotional themes are highly specific and, over time, identifiable, just as they are dynamic and context-driven. These themes organize and impart emotional meaning to what otherwise would be unformulated, insignificant, or inconsequential emotional impressions. Unlike phenomenological description, they generally are not considered as aspects of one's experiential world until arrived at and reflected upon through a *communitarian dialogue* (Orange 1995) centered on a spirit of inquiry and interpretation. Thus, when we speak of one's emotional themes, of the patterning of one's historical and contemporary relationships, or of the dynamic and often implicit processes of affect regulation, we are speaking in the domain of interpretive understanding.

The third level of discourse, *metaphysical/explanatory assumptions*, is less content-organized and more concept- and process-oriented. It refers to one's foundational (sometimes unconscious) assumptions about how things work, to one's convictions about the underpinnings and origination of emotional experience and meaning. An example would be the assumption that all human experiencing and meaning-making is inextricably embedded in a larger world context or complex system of which each of us is but a part. Another related example, quite familiar to us by now, is the assumption that such experiencing and meaning-making can never be attributed solely to one's past, to one's present, or to one's imagined future and that the proportion of these influences will remain forever indeterminate. Speaking on the level of metaphysical assumptions, as the term is employed here, does not address the nature of individual experience or the themes that organize it but rather references the broad universal presuppositions—our convictions about the way things work—that organize the contents and processes of the previous two realms of discourse. The "philosophical unconscious" (Stolorow & Orange 2003, p. 518) is another term that aptly describes this third level of discourse. Distinguishing among these three levels of discourse is not only crucial in subverting conflation and muddle in conversations about psychoanalytic theory but also is an essential attitudinal ingredient implicated in the emergence of therapeutic action in psychoanalysis and psychotherapy. Much of human emotional pain and strife, or alternatively, emotional and relational numbness and complacency resulting in the narrowing of one's affective horizons, is attributable to the ubiquitous, felt discrepancies among these three levels of discourse.

8 Conundrum of personal situatedness, emotional responsibility, and potential (finite) freedom

This attitude encourages us to consider that we humans are thrown (Heidegger 1927) into life circumstances that are largely not of our making, that we often simply discover ourselves in emotional and relational circumstances, sometimes painfully so, that leave us with that sense of *well, how did I get here?*—that feeling of, to paraphrase the Talking Heads (1980), this is not what I designed or intended for myself! How *did* I get here? It also encourages us then to consider assuming responsibility for where indeed we do find ourselves and to accept, without sliding into defeat and a malignant sense of fatedness (Strenger 1998), our current situatedness—to really own it. This attitude then invites us to consider what potential, though finite, freedom we might garner from our current life situation. How might we author our own lives now, moving forward in time? What might we make of ourselves, given what we have been handed and given that we are quintessentially creative beings with the capacity to reflect and imagine? Alternatively stated, this is an attitude of appreciating a sense of constraint in concert with the potential for future self-authorship and self-ownership, akin to what Butler (2004), in regard to gender, refers to as "improvisation within a scene of constraints" (p. 1). Through a sociocultural lens, Butler states it well:

> My agency does not consist in denying this condition of my constitution [of our being contextually determined beings]. If I have any agency, it is opened up by the fact that I am constituted by a social world I never chose. That my agency is riven with paradox does not mean it is impossible. It means only that paradox is a condition [one among others] of its possibility. (p. 3)

Indeed, what brings many of our patients to the consultation room is the anguish of finding oneself in an emotional situatedness that is felt to be either too painful to bear (e.g., traumatic states) and/or felt to be not of one's authorship or ownership (e.g., relational compliance and accommodation [Brandchaft 2007]). This reflects one of the more ironic conundrums of human emotional life—that, phenomenologically and interpretively, we must seize responsibility (i.e., this is my emotional life, this is how I find myself) for that which, explanatorily, could not have been of our own personal making.

As Heidegger (1927) extensively explored, we are thrown into life circumstances over which we have no control and yet in which we may find a life possibility, a potential freedom that our emotional situatedness might offer us. Heidegger referred to this as "finite freedom" (p. 436). Phenomenologically speaking, one's ability to grasp a life possibility that ultimately can be one's own (Sartre 1948) emerges partly out of an awareness of the systemic contexts that have been responsible for determining our situatedness to begin with. In other words, this attitude suggests that, in the absence of a *situational awareness*, included in which is a deepened understanding of the contextual forces (past, present, and imagined future) that conspire to situate us affectively in the very place we find ourselves, we cannot appreciate the extent to which we can exercise what we think of as free will, autonomy, agency, and individuality. Experientially speaking, there can be no doubt of the veracity of states such as autonomy or agency. At the same time, the constitution of these states is entirely systemically and contextually derived!

Assuming these aspects of experience outright, without a previously garnered sense of our fatedness and contextuality, leaves us blind to the forces that have conspired in determining potentially unwanted aspects of our experiential worlds (e.g., emotional convictions about loathsome defects in oneself, or painful and repetitive attributions of traumatic life circumstances to flaws in one's individual mind or psyche). Therapeutically, a broadened awareness of the very contexts— our history, our current state of mind, and our environment—that are implicated in determining where and how we find ourselves offers us life possibilities from which we might choose. Herein lies a potential resolution to, or perhaps dissolution of, dichotomies such as determinism versus free will/autonomy, or self versus no-self. You probably have noticed by now that our seventh and eighth attitudes articulate with one another in essential ways—the seventh providing the underpinnings of and foundation for the eighth.

9 Radical hope

Phrased in the spirit of the work of Jonathan Lear (2007), this attitude essentially speaks to the experience of having hope for a better, imagined future, despite the fact that we may not be able to envision specifically in what form that future might coalesce. It is an appreciation for a reaching out, a longing, for something yet to be discovered and understood. Lear speaks of the "archaic prototype of radical hope: in infancy we are reaching out for sustenance from a source of goodness even though we as yet lack the concepts with which to understand what we are reaching out for" (p. 122). It is an attitude that considers what courage there might be in envisioning something different and positive, despite our inability to picture it clearly in the current moment and despite that older rules, older emotional culture, do not apply anymore. Lear asks: "How is one to face the reality that a way of facing reality is coming to an end?" (p. 133). This type of question may yield answers, over time, given our understanding that complex systems are not rule-driven or predetermined but are quite literally open to change in ways that we may not yet be able to imagine. In this sense, a complexity sensibility inherently offers an abiding radical hope and even an anticipation that one's current state and life circumstance are never permanent and that change is possible in ways yet unenvisioned. Not knowing now how I might feel differently, or how I might reinvent myself, need not preclude me from doing so.

10 Spirit of inquiry[6] / Hermeneutics of trust[7]

This attitude, certainly not originating from complexity theory, is nevertheless quintessentially representative of psychoanalytic complexity and thus deserving of emphasis. That is because a complexity sensibility argues that when change is about to occur, we can never really know how that change will appear and/ or whether it will be useful change at that. Keeping an open attitude of curiosity and thus inquiry (not to be confused with grilling your patient with questions!)

encourages anticipating surprise and appreciating novelty—that sense conveyed to others that we can never know what will emerge next, nor can we ever know, before we get there, what emotional experiences and corresponding meanings may be in store for us. Orange's (2011) hermeneutics of trust resonates well with a true spirit of inquiry in that it conveys to the patient that we are here to discover, together, the emergence of unique emotional life and to be open to surprise, as opposed to assuming we know, more or less, what already resides in the experiential world of the patient and that the patient is usually intent on deceiving us. This attitude also conveys to the patient that we, as analysts and therapists, are more interested in understanding than we are in effecting a specific emotional-behavioral change or developmental trajectory. Lichtenberg et al. (2002) elaborate at length the centrality of a spirit of inquiry:

> Unlike direct questioning and probing, a spirit of inquiry is a guiding *attitude* [my italics], a world view that unites analysts across a spectrum of theories. A spirit of inquiry establishes an ambiance that persists when direct exploratory efforts are prevented by enactments and overwhelming affect states. A spirit of inquiry provides vitality to the psychoanalytic search for subjective and intersubjective awareness. (p. 2)

Indeed, a spirit of inquiry is essential to our clinical work.

Clarice and Me: An Overview

When Clarice arrived at my office on a cold and blustery January day (well, admittedly, yes, it was in Los Angeles, but it was still pretty cold), she slowly and tentatively unbuttoned her wool coat in a manner suggesting the unwrapping of a package whose contents were sure to be unwelcome if not toxic. An attractive woman of thirty-six years, she proceeded to speak of a five-year romantic relationship, still ongoing, the essential problems of which centered, she felt, on her excruciating inability to determine the source of her intense ambivalence and equivocation about being close to him. Specifically, her principal preoccupation appeared to be her inability to assess whether the relationship difficulties were, essentially, her fault, due to her presumed personality defects, or whether they were attributable to the glaring flaws that resided in the partner whom she had chosen. Either way, she was to blame. I suddenly pictured her in a steel box with small openings at the top, just enough for a little breathing room. I wanted to be in there with her, and then I didn't. I myself am prone to claustrophobia. I commented, and she readily agreed, that either perspective rendered her completely responsible for her relationship predicament, given that, in the event it rested with his being the owner of the intransigent flaws, her having chosen this man to begin with, and accommodating to him, was serving as yet another, alternative confirmation of her own defects and perceptual disabilities. The source of her general life-long dysfunction (i.e., anxiety, depression, substance abuse, etc.) and now her relationship woes and uncertainties resided in her mind—she did feel she was the root cause. Her history did not help the situation. By the age of six, Clarice had developed a synesthesia-like condition in which the sound of her parents' breathing or chewing gum (both of which I happen to like to do) would cause her painful skin sensations accompanied by intense agitation and anxiety. Sadly, her complaints about these sensations were met with bewilderment, anger, and demands that she keep her feelings to herself. The problem was *hers* and hers alone. As she grew into adolescence, she found some relief and temporary solace in drug abuse and in accommodating to the sexual dictates of one boyfriend after another. She also found some relief in occasionally cutting herself. Could I fix her or somehow cure her of her defects? Immediately I sensed an impending disjunction between us when I suggested that perhaps there were additional factors in her history, in her environment, and in her life in general that might be contributing to her suffering. At that moment, I felt one of my own attitudes, or emotional convictions—that of the contextuality of all emotional experience, meanings, and corresponding organizing principles—slamming abruptly into hers. At my suggestion, she gazed at me with incredulity and promptly corrected me about the source of her despair. It was all in her head—there most certainly *was* something defective about her. And yes, she said, she had made bad choices. She was the owner and author of her distress and of the trail of dismembered relationships she had left in her wake. And, of course, she was responsible for her synesthesia-like episodes. This was a foundational theme—one that we articulated and reflected on over the course of several years—whose philosophical underpinnings rest in the realm of questions about the origination, ongoing authorship, and presumed ownership of one's experiential world.

Clarice, as an adult, would undergo brief, sudden dissociative episodes in which she would awaken in the night, locate a knife or razor, and begin cutting herself. We came to understand these frightening and disturbing events as two-sided: one side in which her behavior, consciously dissociated as it was, was aimed at accommodating to the demands of others that she disavow, or cut out, aspects of her emotional world—her pain, her reactions to others, her emotional suffering presumed to be self-originated; and, paradoxically, the other side in which she was attempting actually to free herself from the very dictates of authority (Brandchaft 2007) that waged these demands for self-destruction in the first place. Her cutting aimed to excise her unwelcome and unwanted emotions, on the one hand, while it provided one potential avenue by which to instill feelings in and enliven what she frequently experienced as her deadened, dissociated soul, on the other hand. For some time, recognizing and appreciating both sides of this predicament—the requirement of taking sole responsibility for her emotional life and attempting to obliterate it, alongside her nascent and burgeoning (albeit frightening!) efforts to loosen its grip—were intensely challenging for both of us. Obviously I didn't want her to be cutting herself. How do I discourage self-destructive acts while supporting a key facet of the spirit behind them—what appeared to be her sole, nascent effort at grasping a life of her own? Clarice asked me early on, "So, Doc, where do you stand on suicide?" I had immediately felt caught in the conundrum of knowing that potential suicide, on one hand, ultimately was the one thing that truly belonged to her, that was *hers* alone, and that I dare not attempt to take *that* away from her, too, while also knowing, on the other hand, how doggedly confirmed I was in protecting and preserving her life. This encapsulated the ongoing interplay of the complicated conjunctions and disjunctions that lived between us. At that time, I had immediately shared with her my conundrum, which I felt might have been hers as well.

As an overview, despite my personal and clinical propensity toward a complexity sensibility and its attendant contextualist attitudes, my essential, conscious aim in my work with Clarice, as best as I can determine, was to investigate collaboratively the details of her experience of her defectiveness, her apparently self-destructive behaviors, and her experience of her personal corresponding world that continually disappointed her and that was, more or less, presumably of her own making. And despite the overall spirit of inquiry that I believed we both brought to the table and that informed much of our work together, my more implicit attitudes doubtless crept into our exploratory dialogue as, of course, did hers. She sensed, knew, that I felt differently about the authorship and ownership of her personal experience, beliefs, and emotional convictions. She knew I felt quite disturbed by her efforts at self-obliteration, while I remained deeply committed to her efforts toward true agency and emotional freedom. Themes of accommodation and compliance (Brandchaft 2007) became increasingly evident as our work progressed, themes, we discovered, in which she had been held responsible not solely for her own painful affect but for that of others as well. Over time, Clarice began to feel that perhaps she was not as utterly responsible for her sense of her self and the ways she interacted with others as she had been led to believe and that, furthermore, there were indeed forces in her life, past and present, that conspired to shape her emotional life (the *phenomenological*) and the organizing themes (the *interpretive*) underlying them. This emerged through the exploration of those forces and living with the authentic attitudes underlying such an exploration. In other words, her phenomenology began to expand to include the contextuality of her emotional experience. And given my attitudes about the sources of and responsibility for one's emotional life, I cannot exclude the possibility that her shift in perspective to what I think of as a more contextualist frame of mind was yet another act of accommodation on her part—this time to me, as opposed to the traumatogenic others in her past. This concern remains for the two of us to ponder and articulate, and indeed the freedom to do so might in and of itself stand as a distinguishing feature between a pathological accommodation (Brandchaft 2007) and a conscious, useful one. That said, Clarice and I did arrive at a reflective, conscious sense of our colliding attitudes about the origins of emotional experience and the degree to which we may or may not be responsible for it. And this was done through the lens of our seventh and eighth attitudes under consideration. Let's examine for a moment the interface between Clarice's initial attitudes and those derived from a psychoanalytic complexity perspective.

Initially, Clarice understood her experience of herself and her relational world as emanating from herself, from her defects and flaws in particular (about which she felt excruciating shame). She understandably took her felt experiences (phenomenological description) at face value, relegating them to the level of metaphysical/explanatory assumption; "I feel responsible for my state, therefore I *am* responsible for it." Previously she had not taken into consideration the organizing themes that shaped her experience (interpretative understanding) nor the fact that emotional experience is the result of interpretive activity (Gentile 2007, 2008, 2010), as opposed simply to observing and recording the presumably objective truth and reality of the world. Neither had she considered the metaphysical assumptions of a complexity perspective that hold all emotional experience, including our underlying organizing themes, is inextricably embedded in a larger context of which each of us is but a part and that such experience is always informed by one's history, one's current state of mind, and one's environment—the lines of demarcation among which are dynamic and can never be clearly drawn. I believe grasping the distinctions between these three levels of discourse—phenomenological description, interpretive understanding, and metaphysical/explanatory assumptions—and their relationship to one another proved mutative for Clarice. I also believe that her considering this perspective over time did not emerge via education or persuasion but rather through her sensing my implicit attitudes about these ideas in the context of my fundamentally attempting to explore collaboratively her emotional world and emotional convictions. I think she felt that I was more interested in exploration and in establishing an emotional connection with her—that I actually cared about her—than I was in her adopting my complexity-informed attitudes but, of course, I can never be certain about that.

Our eighth attitude, buttressed by our seventh, played an essential role for Clarice as well. Initially, Clarice felt that she was the author and owner of her emotional experience and of her life context in general. When things went wrong, it was her fault. She was not quagmired in the familiar "What did I do to deserve this?" or the "Why do bad things always happen to me?" perspective. Reflecting a variation on the Heideggerian (1927) theme of *thrownness*, Clarice's sense of her self and her life was that *she* had thrown, and continued to throw, herself into an emotional situatedness in which, though felt to be entirely of her own making, she remained hopelessly and powerlessly embedded. Paradoxically, she had little sense of control or authorship over that which she felt she alone had already authored. Clarice's conundrum of accommodatively and prematurely having had to assume personal responsibility for her emotional life and behavior, on one hand, and her relentless conviction that she would forever remain powerlessly confined in that sense of responsibility, on the other hand, remained a substantial source of anguish and perplexity for her. Seemingly paradoxical (Butler 2004), it wasn't until she began to consider that a variety of other sources (our third and eighth attitudes), in addition to herself, had conspired to place her in her current emotional situatedness that she was able to begin considering what freedom, if any at all, might be garnered from the possibilities (Heidegger 1927; Sartre 1948) that she had been given (our eighth attitude). In this instance, Clarice's increased situational awareness of her context-embeddedness—that she is but one constituent of a larger relational system—helped facilitate a greater tendency toward thinking about possibilities that could become *her* possibilities. For Clarice, that meant in part that she could begin understanding her life (and relationship) circumstances as being not entirely of her making and thus reconsider her sense of guilt and shame for all that she previously felt she had authored on her own. Over time, we discovered that her decreased sense of guilt and shame liberated her to be more proactive in reversing many of her relationship decisions (i.e., she didn't feel as much of that sense of "Well, you've made your bed, and now you have to lie in it!"). In this instance, at least for Clarice, grasping a life possibility of her own actually meant relinquishing a complete, overarching, and archaic sense of emotional responsibility, repudiating a parental surround in which indeed she had been held responsible for all her apparent distress and seeming emotional aberrations. The responsibility for emotional experience and life circumstances became, *phenomenologically*, distributed across multiple individuals and life contexts, which, *explanatorily*, is where they had always resided.

In this clinical instance, like many that we clinicians undergo, a spirit of inquiry into Clarice's emotional life and its corresponding meanings inevitably led to a deepening of our understanding of the contexts—past, present, and imagined future—that were and are responsible for such life to begin with. Often, this deepening entails an appreciation for the relationship between felt experience and the greater interpenetrating relational systems that give rise to it and for a corresponding sense that, to a significant degree, we consequently are largely not the authors and owners of our personal emotional worlds and their embedded situatedness. In the metaphysical/explanatory sense, there is no free will, individuality, or personal agency. How could there be? In the phenomenological sense, the degree to which we may experience free will and personal agency nevertheless always remains context-dependent. Furthermore, the idea that we are not the authors and owners of our personal affectivity and situatedness need not slide into constructivist assumptions that there are no real entities, no individual persons to be discovered, no life directions to be authored and owned (Frie & Coburn 2011). Instead of eliminating the concept of individual minds, for instance, from our psychoanalytic armamentarium, a psychoanalytic complexity perspective helps us contextualize those minds in broadening our understanding of the sources and origins of our emotional experience. This proves to be a useful corrective to the wide swing of the modernist/postmodernist pendulum found in deconstructionism. An acknowledgment of and appreciation for the relationship between the three different dimensions of discourse help subvert the endless obsession with dichotomizing modernist and postmodernist views of the self and self-narrative. Additionally, coming to appreciate our embeddedness in a larger world context for which we cannot be held responsible—but for which we must ultimately take responsibility—is an essential constituent in the potential for garnering a personal sense of freedom, of agency, and of what is felt to be true and real.

Clarice and Me: Attitudes and Engagement

In addition to a spirit of curiosity and inquiry, a variety of complexity-informed attitudes—several that have been in evidence here—were clinically instrumental in helping Clarice expand a sense of her unbidden personal situatedness, on one hand, and of a potential for developing alternate organizing principles and courageously engaging a sense of finite freedom, on the other hand. At moments, we might feel quite literally thrown into life, while simultaneously we also might engage in, at least, thinking about how we might choose to expand forward in different, creative, and perhaps heretofore unenvisioned life trajectories. This was certainly the case with Clarice. As we witnessed earlier in my description of my experience and relationship with Jack in Chapter 1, it is essential to be able to identify when a system is lively, energetic, and poised for change, just as it is vital to hold hope in contexts of hopelessness (Winnicott 1986). In this next clinical segment, it seemed to me that the action of two particular attitudes operated in the foreground and, ultimately, was mutative. The attitudes were (1) valuing attempting to sense the presence of an alive, dynamic system, and (2) valuing emergent affective change as a source of increased hope for positive growth in the face of repetition and darkness. These attitudes correspond with facets of our fifth and ninth attitudes, respectively, and partly rest on the complexity proposition that disequilibrium, dynamism, and uncertainty are the pulse of life and that equilibrium, resolution, and complacency are tantamount to death.

In the previous section, we explored from an overview the role of the attitude that emotional life and emotional development are emergent properties of a larger, complex relational system—the attitude that we thus *find ourselves* inextricably embedded in a larger relational life context (for which we cannot be entirely responsible but for which we nevertheless might come to assume responsibility). Herein lies the difference between *being* and *assuming*, meaning that whereas we cannot be completely responsible for our current life situatedness—the *how-one-finds-oneself-ness* of which Heidegger (1927) speaks—we nevertheless have to assume responsibility for where and how we find ourselves if we are to move ahead and realize other life possibilities, other means of grasping freedom and creativity. Another attitude, and equally essential, was that things do not always work the way they may feel they do. I may feel I am solely responsible for my experiential world, that my own single brain is determining the sum total of my emotional experience and the meanings I attribute to it but, of course, that is not the case. There is no brain without culture and context (Shane & Carlton 2009). Or, I may feel I am not at all responsible and have no say in things, that I am a product solely of my socio-historical-cultural context. And, of course, that is not the case either. I am a reflexive being with a sense of individuality and direction (well, on a good day!). There is no culture or context without brain. As we have seen, these themes were quite pivotal in Clarice's development, not the least of which was a loosening of her deeply ensconced presumption that all her problems were her fault—a result of an essential flaw deeply embedded in her psyche alone—about which she had felt enormous shame and guilt.

When Clarice first arrived at my office, she anticipated unleashing a toxicity that neither of us could tolerate. As it turned out, the contents were not quite as toxic as she or I had anticipated. For some time, however, many of her emotional convictions frequently collided with my own, as did mine with hers. Eventually Clarice and I arrived at a reflective, conscious sense of our discrepant attitudes about the origins of emotional experience and the degree to which we may or may not be responsible for it. She certainly knew where I stood on these issues, and she also knew that I knew where *she* stood. Our attitudes about her life and our relationship became quite articulable over time. They became a source of conflict, disagreement, engagement, and play between us. However, perhaps more importantly, Clarice was developing a self-valuing voice, one that reflected now an unwillingness to *be* responsible for all things. She *was*, however, beginning to *assume* responsibility for her life situatedness, to take more ownership of her life.

A few years into treatment, several facets of our relationship particularly stood out in my mind. One was a dawning awareness that she was beginning to enjoy an increased courage to own and express her own voice, her having successfully distributed her sense of responsibility for her life situations across a larger relational matrix, including, more recently, me. At times, I experienced myself as segmented and in conflict about these changes; I felt predominantly celebratory for her, for us, while sometimes also strangely on edge, frightened at what her new-found agency and emotional expressiveness would bring vis-à-vis our relationship. On the edges of my experience, I was vaguely aware of the potential for being attacked for something—I wasn't sure what—for which I didn't want to be held responsible. I found this exceedingly ironic. We had had plenty of disagreements and a few arguments centered on the discrepancy between our emotional convictions and a plethora of resulting conversations about our engagement around those disagreements. I was certainly used to her being angry with me, and our relationship was deepening, but I sensed something different on the horizon, and it was making me anxious. This led to a gradual, at-first-implicit diminishment of my emotional availability and emotional honesty (honesty with myself *and* with her). Her decreased sense of shame and self-blame emboldened her to challenge me in increasingly uncomfortable ways, and I was protecting myself. In particular, as she became increasingly aware of her dependency on me, she also became angry about the asymmetry of our relationship. She needed me; I didn't need her. She loved me; I didn't love her. She was attached to me; she could come and go as far as I was concerned—it wouldn't matter to me. Oh, and then there was the little detail that I was charging her money. She had to pay for my attention, and I certainly could live without *her* attention. These apparent inequities revived aspects of my own historical, at times traumatic, familial demands that *I* had experienced early in life. These demands, as I experienced them, were about others requiring me to feel how *they* felt, not to feel themselves how they could not allow themselves to feel, and to manage their emotional lives in ways that centered on the need to obliterate that sense of asymmetry inherent in, and so crucial to, parent-child relationships. The penalty for rejecting these parental demands felt, to me, like a catastrophic severing of my ties to those on whom I relied.

Trying not to argue truth and reality presumptions, I listened and explored what, exactly, in her view was informing her impressions of our relationship and also how it was for her to dare to express them to me. She felt I hardly had to lift as much as a finger to keep the relationship going—she was doing all the work. And she was the one who had to endure the time between sessions, during which time I probably didn't even think about her. In general, she just didn't feel a sense of mutual, intimate connection and engagement, which, notably, she now felt she wanted and deserved. She was worth it. And she also didn't want to perpetuate her feeling of being so much at the mercy of the other. As she became more demanding for signs that I really cared about her, often in an angry kind of way, I became more silent and a bit withdrawn—that *deer in the headlights* kind of feeling. I simultaneously knew—witnessed before my very eyes—how much I was contributing to a rapidly spiraling impasse, one in which her desperation for connection and my now-not-surprising emotional withdrawal intertwined. Of course, my own history, my own current state of mind, and my own environment were informing the alterations in my responsiveness to her. My own trauma-based, dissociative response to angry demands for that which I could not provide and/or wished not to provide would revive her more archaic shame states—states that our prior work together had attenuated substantially. This pattern, with its increasing intensity, remained more implicit and unarticulated for a number of weeks, culminating in one pivotal session in which she stomped out of my office in response to my ending the session with one of my "I have to stop for now" type of comments. Rarely had I experienced before the acute anger that one's footsteps alone—over carpet, no less—could convey in such a palpable way. She felt shamed and quite angry. She left me rather shaken and a bit despairing, with my knowing especially how much her current environment—that, in part, included me!—was contributing to her increasing sense of desperation and shame. This resonated with aspects of my own emotional world in which historically I had found angry, seething, silent withdrawals in my familial surround to be the harbinger of trauma and disaster.

And now I too sat with shame, and anxiety. I imagined what I might say to a supervisee in a situation like this: Upon her return to your office, inquire about her experience of the last session, particularly the ending of it, track her affect, see what comes to life between you, and respond! Do not just sit there like a frozen deer about to get whacked by a Mack truck. Do not make some kind of intellectualized genetic interpretation. In fact, you might want to skip the naïve "Tell me what your experience was that made you so angry so quickly" type of inquiry and just get to the point. Perhaps something like: "I haven't been my usual self lately [whatever *that* is], and I think you're feeling that and reacting to that. Lately I haven't been meeting you where I've asked *you* to meet *me*. I've found myself withdrawing." Perhaps the grip of her shame, as well as mine, and sense of rejection might loosen, and perhaps she might experience me as beginning to reconnect and to meet her. Perhaps this could be a moment of heightened complexity for us both.

But no! Instead, I began the next session with my antlers firmly in place, while she, somewhat to my surprise, began a litany of apologies for her angry enactment at the end of the previous session. My heart dropped. We were losing another opportunity to transform a traumatically accommodative, repetitive system into a transformative one (Lachmann 2008). The point of self-criticality, or *tipping point*, had receded back into a system that was, once again, too ordered and not reflected on. D. N. Stern (2004) writes of *now moments*. For me, this felt much more like a *now or never moment*. I replied that I wished to reject her apology, that though she had not been using words, she had angrily announced herself, loudly and clearly, and that I would not want to miss out on her taking a stand and speaking her voice. My sadness for what was about to be entirely lost—for what had been woefully lost for her historically in her having had to accommodate to those around her—helped extract the antlers from my head and join her in her courage for insisting on connection and engagement. She brightened, and said, "Well, yes, I am pretty pissed. I don't want to have to be in a relationship again where I'm always clawing around the edges, begging for a connection. Been there, done that." Indeed, she had been there, she had done that. In the weeks that followed and with no small amount of anxiety, we continued this heightened level of engagement. "If you feel like withdrawing," she announced, "for God's sake, why don't you just say so!" I replied, "Indeed, why the hell not?" We were able to sustain, at least for a while, this sense of aliveness and vitality in our exchanges—importantly, ones in which she was making herself matter. The feel of our system became, once again, more dynamic, messy, noisy, and alive, reflecting the signs of a complex system in action. And we were learning to recognize what a dyadic system—ours in particular—feels like when it is moving somewhere.

Weeks later, our conversation drifted away and then back again to our relationship, as it often did. In the midst of one of these exchanges, she jolted me with the question: "Well, do you care about me?" Surprised, I said to her that I thought that was an unusual question, considering that I suspected she may already know the answer. I said that I thought that perhaps her question was more reflective of another instance of her making herself matter, and of her asserting that she was worth it. Smiling, she agreed, and also said, "Yeah, I know you care about me—I think you care about me lots, despite that I'm the one doing all the thinking about you and you aren't necessarily thinking about me that much." "Yes," I replied, "more inequities between us." She nodded, and there was a brief pause. I then asked, with tongue firmly planted in cheek, "Well, I'm curious, what is it exactly that makes you think I care about you so much?" She glared at me piercingly. After a weighty pause, we chortled and then went silent again. Then, in a more serious tone, she said, "Well, what about sex?" Pensive and trying to buy time, I finally replied, "Well...what *about* sex?" More silence, then I said,

"Well, under the right circumstances, I highly recommend it." "Ha!" she said, "...don't worry, I'm just fucking with you." I replied, "Well then, I guess there's all kinds of fucking and ways to be intimate and engaged, aren't there? And I guess there are some ways we can know each other and others ways we can't." "Yes, of course, I know that's not possible, and what good would you be to me then, if we did have sex?" Moved by her comment, I replied, "Indeed, what good then?" And to myself I silently interpreted, here is your self-valuing voice again Clarice—I like that! I felt quite moved by this particular exchange, and Clarice seemed more comfortable with it than I did. And good for her! And what was my discomfort about anyway? More personal guilt and shame, and reverberating trauma, about the inequities of this relationship? Some themes simply persist. This exchange reflects another instance of novelty, emergence, and play for both of us—another example of autocatalysm in action. Who is the agent of change here? And when and where did the change begin? As I mentioned before, we were both learning, experientially, the difference between a repetitive system and a transformative system (Lachmann 2000) and would in the future continue to seek out the dynamic, edge-of-chaos type of engagement that we had come to be able to identify. In *that* sense, we were both on the same page. And I was wondering, what would be next? Perhaps something like, "Well, so, do you at least find me attractive?" but it remains to be seen what will emerge next. We can never predict. Probably nothing good, though, will come to life without dynamism and anxiety. And thus did our relationship progress and oscillate from play to disagreement to intimacy to despair to loss to affection to distance and to play again, month after month, year after year—now recognizable attractor states frequently in motion.

How might we think about the attitudes here that may have been especially formative and mutative in this clinical snapshot? One attitude in evidence here, so central to clinical practice—that of valuing the emergence of what feels like something new and useful in the patient's and therapist's respective experiential worlds—pertains to the presumption that we humans, given a responsive enough relational context, tend to expand and grow in useful and adaptive ways (Kohut 1977, 1984; Lichtenberg et al. 1996; Shane 2006; Tolpin 2002, 2007) and that, clinically speaking, such adaptive growth is encouraged through the acknowledgement and articulation of those at-times subtle developmental tendrils (Tolpin 2002, 2007) that otherwise might dissolve back into an emotionally indistinct, undifferentiated oblivion. Determining the nature and presence of an emergent, developmental advance, including distinguishing it from what otherwise might be maladaptive and/or repetitive phenomena, is not necessarily easy. It requires a sensitivity to the nuances of an ever-changing context and to the corresponding meanings associated with the emergence of novel affective experience and behavior. Alternatively stated, what is emergent, novel, and developmental for one person might easily be apparent regression and destruction for another. (Clarice's apology might be misconstrued by some as development and maturity—but in my view, it most certainly was not.)[8]

Of equal therapeutic consequence, however, is the impact of the implicit attitudes conveyed to the patient in the course of acknowledging and articulating individual and dyadic developmental advances. Such acknowledgement and articulation not only draw attention to the system's growth—certainly vital for the patient to know about, to learn how eventually to recognize on her own—but convey that, yes, life can move forward in positive directions; yes, not all experience is trauma and loss; yes, not all relational interactions need to be organized around accommodation (Brandchaft 2007), self-suppression, or self-destruction. This vital, additional attitude conveys hope in the sense explored by Lear (2007), in which he defines true courage as sustaining a *radical hope* for adaptive change and expanded freedom in the face of uncertainty and ambiguity as to what form, exactly, that change and expansion will take. To have one's novel, emergent affective experience brought to one's attention is also to hear that one's interlocutor feels that development *can* happen, that it is valued and worth looking for, that being relentlessly open to play and banter is essential, and that perhaps there is more to come.

Notes

1 'Once In A Lifetime' words and music by Brian Eno, David Byrne, Christopher Frantz, Jerry Harrison and Tina Weymouth. Copyright © 1980 by EG Music Ltd., WB Music Corp. and Index Music, Inc. All Rights for EG Music Ltd. in the United States and Canada Administered by Universal Music–MGB Songs All Rights for Index Music, Inc. Administered by WB Music Corp.International Copyright Secured. All Rights Reserved. Reprinted by permission of Hal Leonard Corporation.
2 Sartre, J.-P. (1948). *Being and Nothingness*, trans. H. E. Barnes, New York, NY: Philosophical Library, pp. 267–8. Copyright Philosophical Library, Inc., New York.
3 I thank Estelle Shane for pointing out this reference to me.
4 I am reminded here of Proust's (2003) observation that "[p]erhaps the immobility of the things around us is imposed on them by our certainty that they are themselves and not anything else, by the immobility of our mind confronting them" (p. 6).
5 These particular designations were arrived at in dialogue with Robert Stolorow in which we began discussing the distinction between the levels of discourse of phenomenology and of explanation. After some discussion, it became evident that a refinement and elaboration of these distinctions were necessary; the three terms were intersubjectively derived and remain of ambiguous origin.
6 Kohut 1984; Lichtenberg, Lachmann, & Fosshage 1992, 2002; Mitchell 2000; Stolorow & Atwood 1992.
7 Orange 2011.
8 Developmental or forward-edge tendrils need not be relegated to one individual. Complex systems have their development tendrils as well, and we need to remain alert to them, as both Clarice and I attempted to do.

Chapter 6

Conclusion

What shall we call our "self?" Where does it begin? Where does it end? It overflows into everything that belongs to us—and then it flows back again.
—Henry James[1]

Once a complexity sensibility has been studied, obsessed about, then studied some more, and then *felt* to be part of one's sense of self, there really is no turning back. At least that has been my experience. I will never picture biological evolution, the flow of human dialogue, a flock of starlings over Scotland, or the machinations of our universe in the same way, nor can I any longer imagine the vicissitudes of emotional life and meaning-making through the more traditional scientistic lens that was the basis of my initial educational and professional indoctrination. Experientially speaking, selfhood and worldhood may seem quite fragmented, segmented, particularized, disjointed, and/or otherwise reduced down and rendered into parts and things. However, explanatorily speaking, all things, all people, are relentlessly and irrevocably connected and intertwined in ways we can never fully know. The unique fabric of earthly life binds us all—historically, socially, culturally, and ritualistically. What my grandmother, who, horribly, once forced me to drink prune juice, said to me when I was five years old will impact my patient's five-year-old grandson next week. What *his* grandson said to him last week will impact me and what I say to my next patient in the next hour. When we can comprehend our selfhood and worldhood as quintessentially dynamic, fluid, unpredictable, powerfully relationally distributed (not encased in a cranial shell), and as neither rule-driven nor pre-designed, things change, and I think for the better. This book, our thought experiment about complexity and attitudes, reflects an initial foray into a play space that I hope will continue to expand in evocative and useful directions.

Ultimately, psychoanalytic complexity does not, in the technical sense, *get applied.* Attending to and valuing the emergence of one's personal metaphors while listening to a patient's dream, for instance, and then consequently formulating interpretations and perhaps other interventions in response to those metaphors, might be an example of applying a specific technique. Such a technique privileges the use of metaphor and perhaps sharing it and its implications with the patient. Or, if the clinician happens to value understanding a patient's anxiety states, as opposed to leaping to ameliorate them, some form of inquiry and danger analysis might ensue. In these instances, the clinician's underlying presumptions, or *attitudes*, inform what gets said and done next. In many circumstances, explicit theory informs conscious technique. In contrast, psychoanalytic complexity, as it has evolved thus far, emphasizes the fact that its sensibility comes with a host of attitudes and that those attitudes, in and of themselves, exert substantial influences that reverberate throughout the clinical relationship, and beyond. Those influences may appear in the form of specific clinical techniques, retrospectively examined, but such techniques, when they coalesce in the clinical moment, are not the result of previously designed, outlined, and/or codified interventions based on a theoretical perspective. Rather, they are left to the clinician to decide about in real time. Ideally, these decisions emanate from the clinician's being *herself*—her personal *clinical-self*. And thus, if complexity theory can be said to be *applied* in any explicit fashion, it is through a close study and pondering of its tenets and then through placing them aside and letting them rest in the realm of the implicit. If a particular theory has been studied thoroughly enough and, in some respects, deemed worthwhile, it will be engaged and activated clinically without explicit thought and in the absence of conscious, intellectualized maneuvering. In this vein, I find myself repeatedly drawn to Ghent's (1990) elegant concept of *surrender*. He states,

> [Surrender] convey[s] a quality of liberation and expansion of the self as a corollary to the letting down of defensive barriers…Surrender is not a voluntary activity…It is an experience of being "in the moment," totally in the present, where past and future, the two tenses that require "mind" in the sense of secondary processes, have receded from consciousness. (pp. 108–111)

For me, *surrender*, following Ghent (1990), is a kind of *finding oneself being oneself*. And this is what we clinicians hope for, for ourselves and for our patients, in working psychoanalytically.

An essential aim of this work has been to explore yet another part of the complexity elephant and to grasp more robustly the influential role of the underlying attitudes that necessarily permeate the clinical relationship or any relationship, for that matter—*whatever* those attitudes might be. In that light, it bears emphasizing that the analyst's attitudes, say her attitudes about the highly distributed nature of emotional experience, the origins and future impact of which is relentlessly spread throughout a much larger relational matrix, are not necessarily experienced by the patient in the manner in which they are felt by the analyst. However complexity-derived, well meaning, or compassionate the analyst's attitudes may be, they frequently may not be experienced as such by the patient; intersubjective disjunctions abound. Suggesting to Clarice that she may not be the sole, responsible author of her emotional and external life situatedness often, for her, was felt to be a confirmation of her emotional conviction that she, and her way of perceptually organizing the world, was simply wrong—that she was, indeed, flawed and defective. This brings to mind Mitchell's (1997) explication of the bootstrap problem, in which attempts at interpreting the organizing themes that inform the patient's experiential world are often themselves immediately assimilated as confirmations of those very themes. In these instances, the conundrum simply (though not easily) must be lived with and articulated. This also articulates with Aron's (2006) response to the problem of polarization of self states (the *seesaw* and *compass* phenomena) and resulting potential impasse in which, ultimately, being able to tolerate and hold highly discrepant and dichotomized perspectives engenders useful, alternative ways of interacting and experiencing one's selfhood and worldhood. It was frequently the case that Clarice and I found struggle *and* passion in voicing our respective, discrepant attitudes, which process, in and of itself, I believe, was mutative for us both. Clinically, disagreement and conflict often contribute to the disequilibrium that is so essential to the survival, maintenance, and flow of a complex human system.

Indeed, much of the clinical exchange involves playing with both the analyst's and the patient's respective set of attitudes. Where this book has highlighted the potential role of the analyst's attitudes, it was not to suggest that that is where the action is. The agent of change is always a systems event. Contrary to traditional thought in psychoanalysis and psychotherapy, the participants, and not one person alone, create the agent of change. Therapeutic action is thus understood as an emergent property and product of the clinical relationship, the medium in which the participant-explorers together can find their own unique passage toward something different than the repetitive, the usual, and the perpetually traumatic. As was addressed in Chapter 1, autocatalytic processes allow for the emergence of something novel and, with hope and anxiety, useful change. Moreover, such novelty and change are distributed across and reverberate throughout the larger relational systems in one's life. It is context, and not a single brain, that gives rise to emotional experience and meaning, and it is throughout one's life context that novelty and change become similarly distributed. In that sense, therapeutic action and change are as much of *ambiguous ownership* as are one's past, present, and future emotional life.

Note

1 James, Henry (1881, 2008) *The Portrait of a Lady,* Volume 1 (of 2), Gutenberg EBook #2833, Produced by Eve Sobol and David Widger, Project Gutenberg.

Bibliography

Abend, S. M. (1989) 'Countertransference and psychoanalytic technique,' *Psychoanalytic Quarterly* 58: 374–395.

Adler, G. (1980) 'Transference, real relationship and alliance,' *International Journal of Psycho-analysis* 61: 547–558.

Ainsworth, M. and Bell, S. (1974) 'Mother-infant interaction and the development of competence.' In J. Connolly and J. Bruner (Eds.), *The Growth of Competence*, New York: Academic Press.

Arnetoli, C. (1999) 'Parallel and sequential working in the intersubjective field.' Paper presented at Multiple Perspectives on Subjectivity Conference, Rome, Italy.

Aron, L. (1996) *A Meeting of Minds: Mutuality in Psychoanalysis*, Hillsdale, NJ: The Analytic Press.

Aron, L. (2000) 'Self-reflexivity and the therapeutic action of psychoanalysis,' *Psychoanalytic Psychology* 17: 667–689.

Aron, L. (2004) 'On: Hans Loewald: A radical conservative,' *International Journal of Psycho-analysis* 85: 530–532.

Aron, L. (2006) 'Analytic impasse and the third: Clinical implications of intersubjectivity,' *International Journal of Psycho-Analysis* 87: 349–368.

Atlan, H. (1984) 'Disorder, complexity, and meaning.' In P. Livingston (Ed.), *Disorder and Order*, Saratoga, CA: Anima Libri.

Atwood, G. E. (2011) *The Abyss of Madness*, New York: Routledge.

Atwood, G. E. and Stolorow, R. D. (1984) *Structures of Subjectivity*, Hillsdale, NJ: The Analytic Press.

Atwood, G. E. and Stolorow, R. D. (2012) 'The demons of phenomenological contextualism: A conversation,' *Psychoanalytic Review* 99: 267–286.

Atwood, G., Orange, D., and Stolorow, R. (2002) 'Shattered worlds/psychotic states: A post-Cartesian view of the experience of personal annihilation,' *Psychoanalytic Psychology* 19: 281–306.

Audi, R. (Ed) (1995) *Cambridge Dictionary of Philosophy*, Cambridge, UK: Cambridge University Press.

Bacal H. A. (1994) 'The analyst's reaction to the analysand's unresponsiveness: A self-psychological view of countertransference.' Paper presented at the University of California, Los Angeles.

Bacal H. A. (2006) 'Specificity theory: Conceptualizing a personal and professional quest for therapeutic possibility,' *International Journal of Psychoanalytic Self Psychology* 1, 2: 133–155.

Bacal H. A. (2011) *The Power of Specificity in Psychotherapy*. New York: Jason Aronson.

Bacal, H. A. and Carlton, L. (2010) 'Kohut's last words on analytic cure and how we hear them now—a view from specificity theory,' *International Journal of Psychoanalytic Self Psychology* 5: 132–143.

Bacal, H. A. and Herzog, B. (2003) 'Specificity theory and optimal responsiveness: An outline,' *Psychoanalytic Psychology* 20: 635–648.

Bacal, H. A. and Thomson, P. G., (1996) 'The psychoanalyst's selfobject needs and the effect of their frustration on the treatment: A new view of countertransference,' *Progress in Self Psychology* 12: 17–35.

Bak, P. (1996) *How Nature Works: The Science of Self-Organized Criticality*, New York: Copernicus.

Balint, A. and Balint, M. (1939) 'On transference and counter-transference,' *International Journal of Psycho-Analysis* 20: 223–230.

Balint, M. (1968) *The Basic Fault*, Evanston, Ill.: Northwestern University Press.

Bateson, G. (1942) 'Some systematic approaches to the study of culture and personality,' *Character and Personality* 11: 76–82.

Baudrillard, J. (1994) *The Illusion of the End*, trans. C. Turner, Stanford, CA: Stanford University Press.

Beebe, B. (2004) 'Faces in relation: A case study,' *Psychoanalytic Dialogues* 14: 1–51.

Beebe, B. (2005) 'Mother-infant research informs mother-infant treatment,' *Psychoanalytic Studies of the Child* 60: 7–46.

Beebe, B., Knoblauch, S., Rustin, J., and Sorter, D. (2003) 'Introduction: A systems view,' *Psychoanalytic Dialogues* 13: 743–775.

Beebe, B. and Lachmann, F. M. (1994) 'Representation and internalization in infancy,' *Psychoanalytic Psychology* 11: 127–165

Beebe, B. and Lachmann, F. M. (1998) 'Co-constructing inner and relational processes: Self and mutual regulation in infant research and adult treatment,' *Psychoanalytic Psychology* 15: 480–516.

Beebe, B. and Lachmann, F. M. (2001) *Infant Research and Adult Treatment: A Dyadic Systems Approach*, Hillsdale, NJ:Analytic Press.

Beebe, B., Lachmann, F. M., and Jaffe, J. (1997) 'Mother-infant interaction structures and presymbolic self and object representations,' *Psychoanalytic Dialogues* 7: 133–182.

Beebe, J. (2001) 'A comment on "What is our age suffering from?" The Schweizer Illustrierte's 1942 interview with C. G. Jung,' *Journal of Analytic Psychology* 46: 365–370.

Benjamin, J. (1998) *Shadow of the Other*, New York: Routledge.

Benjamin, J. (2004) 'Beyond doer and done to: an intersubjective view of thirdness,' *Psychoanalytic Quarterly* 73: 5–46.

Bernstein, R. (1983) *Beyond Objectivism and Relativism: Science, Hermeneutics, and Praxis*. Philadelphia, PA: University of Pennsylvania Press.

Bernstein, J. W. (1999) 'Countertransference: our new royal road to the unconscious?,' *Psychoanalytic Dialogues* 9, 3: 275–299.

Bertalanffy, L. von (1968) *General Systems Theory*, New York: Braziller.

Bion, W. R. (1952) 'Group dynamics: a re-view,' *International Journal of Psycho-Analysis* 33: 235–247.

Bion, W. R. (1959) 'Attacks on linking,' *International Journal of Psycho-Analysis* 40: 308–315.

Bion, W. R. (1967) *Second Thoughts*, New York: Jason Aronson.

Bion, W. R. (1970) *Attention and Interpretation: A Scientific Approach to Insight in Psycho-Analysis and Groups*, London, UK: Tavistock.

Bion, W. R. (1973) *Bion's Brazilian lectures: No. 1*, Sao Paulo, Brazil: Imago Editora.

Bohm, D. (1980) *Wholeness and the Implicate Order*, London: Routledge and Kegan Paul.

Bohr, A. and B. R. Mottelson (1957) *Collective and Individual-Particle Aspects Of Nuclear Structure*, Copenhagen: I kommission hos Munksgaard.

Bohr, N. (1963) *Essays 1958–1962 on Atomic Physics and Human Knowledge*, New York: Interscience Publishers.

Bollas, C. (1987) *The Shadow of The Object*, New York: Columbia University Press.

Bonn, E. (2010) 'Turbulent contextualism: bearing complexity toward change,' *International Journal of Psychoanalytic Self Psychology* 5: 1–18.

Boston Change Process Study Group (2007) 'The foundational level of psychodynamic meaning: implicit process in relation to conflict, defense and the dynamic unconscious,' *International Journal of Psycho-analysis* 88: 843–860.

Bowlby, J. (1969) *Attachment and Loss*, vol. 1, New York: Basic Books.

Bowlby, J. (1973) *Attachment and Loss*, vol. 2, New York: Basic Books.

Bowlby, J. (1980) *Attachment and Loss*, vol. 3, New York: Basic Books.

Brandchaft, B. (1993) 'To free the spirit from its cell.' In A. Goldberg (ed.), *The Widening Scope of Self Psychology*, Northvale, NJ:The Analytic Press.

Brandchaft, B. (2007) 'Systems of pathological accommodation and change in analysis,' *Psychoanalytic Psychology*, 24, 4: 667–687.

Brandchaft, B., Doctors, S., and Sorter, D. (2010) *Toward An Emancipatory Psychoanalysis*, New York: Routledge.

Brenner, C. (1979) 'Working alliance, therapeutic alliance, and transference,' *Journal of the American Psychoanalytic Association* 27S: 137–157.

Breuer, J. and Freud, S. (1893) 'On The psychical mechanism of hysterical phenomena: preliminary communication from studies on hysteria.' In J. Strachey (ed. and trans.) *The Standard Edition of the Complete Psychological Works of Sigmund Freud* (vol. 2), New York: W.W. Norton.

Bromberg, P. M. (1993) 'Shadow and substance: A relational perspective on clinical process,' *Psychoanalytic Psychology* 10: 147–168.

Bromberg, P. M. (1996) 'Standing in the spaces: the multiplicity of self and the psychoanalytic relationship,' *Contemporary Psychoanalysis* 32: 509–535.

Bromberg, P. M. (2001) *Standing in the Spaces: Essays on Clinical Process Trauma and Dissociation*, New York: Routledge.

Bromberg, P. M. (2006) *Awakening The Dreamer: Clinical Journeys*, Mahwah, NJ:The Analytic Press.

Brooks, P. (1994) *Psychoanalysis and Storytelling (Number 10 in the Bucknell Lectures in Literary Theory)*, Cambridge, Mass.: Blackwell.

Brothers, L. (2002) *Mistaken Identity: The Mind-Brain Problem Reconsidered*, New York: SUNY Press.

Buber, M. (1970) *On Intersubjectivity and Cultural Creativity*, Chicago, Ill.: University of Chicago Press.

Buechler, S. (2002) 'Fromm's spirited values and analytic neutrality,' *International Forum of Psychoanalysis* 11: 275–278.

Butler, J. (2004) *Undoing Gender*, New York: Routledge.

Casement, P. (1992) *Learning From the Patient*, New York: Guilford.

Chaitin, G. (1990) *Information, Randomness, and Incompleteness*, Singapore: World Scientific.

Charles, M. (2002) *Patterns: Building Blocks of Experience*, Hillsdale, NJ:Analytic Press.

Cilliers, P. (1998) *Complexity and Postmodernism: Understanding Complex Systems*, New York: Routledge.

Clayton, K. (1998) *Nonlinear Dynamics and Chaos Theory: Application to Psychology*. Unpublished manuscript.

Coburn, W. J. (1997) 'The vision is supervision: Transference-countertransference dynamics and disclosure in the supervision relationship,' *Bulletins of the Menninger Clinic*, 61: 481–494.

Coburn, W. J. (1998) 'Patient unconscious communication and analyst narcissistic vulnerability in the countertransference experience,' *Progress In Self Psychology* 14: 17–31.

Coburn, W. J. (1999) 'Attitudes of embeddedness and transcendence in psychoanalysis: Subjectivity, self-experience and countertransference,' *Journal of The American Academy of Psychoanalysis* 26, 2: 101–119.

Coburn, W. J. (2000) 'The organizing forces of contemporary psychoanalysis: Reflections on nonlinear dynamic systems theory,' *Psychoanalytic Psychology* 17: 750–770.

Coburn, W. J. (2001a) 'Subjectivity, emotional resonance, and the sense of the real,' *Psychoanalytic Psychology* 18: 303–319.

Coburn, W. J. (2001b) 'Transference-countertransference dynamics and disclosure,' In S. Gill (ed.) *The Supervisory Alliance: Facilitating the Psychotherapist's Learning Experience*, Northvale, NJ: Jason Aronson.

Coburn, W. J. (2002) 'A world of systems: the role of systemic patterns of experience in the therapeutic process,' *Psychoanalytic Inquiry* 22, 5: 655–677.

Coburn, W. J. (2006) 'Terminations, self-states and complexity in psychoanalysis: Commentary on paper by Jody Messler Davies,' *Psychoanalytic Dialogues* 16: 603–610.

Coburn, W. J. (2007a) 'Don't drag me around: The phenomenology of complexity in group psychotherapy: Commentary on paper by Robert Grossmark,' *Psychoanalytic Dialogues* 17, 4: 501–512.

Coburn, W. J. (2007b) 'Psychoanalytic complexity: Pouring new wine directly into one's mouth.' In P. Buirski and A. Kottler (Eds.), *New Developments in Self Psychology Practice*, Northvale, NJ: Jason Aronson.

Coburn, W. J. (2007c) 'What is a weeble anyway, and what is a wobble too? A discussion of Phyllis DiAmbrosio's paper, "Weeble Wobbles: Resilience within the Psychoanalytic Situation,"' *International Journal of Psychoanalytic Self Psychology* 2, 4: 463–473.

Coburn, W. J. (2009) 'Attitudes in psychoanalytic complexity: An alternative to postmodernism in psychoanalysis.' In R. Frie and D. Orange (Eds.), *Beyond Postmodernism: New Dimensions in Clinical Theory and Practice*, New York: Routledge.

Coburn, W. J. (2010) Contextualizing individuality and therapeutic action in psychoanalysis and psychotherapy. In R. Frie and W. Coburn (Eds.), *Persons In Context: The Challenge of Individuality in Theory and Practice*, New York: Routledge.

Coburn, W. J. (2011a) 'Psychoanalytic complexity: Context, attitudes and epistemological ineptitude.' Paper presented at the AAPCSW Conference in Marina del Rey, California, March, 2011 and at the International Conference on the Psychology of the Self in Los Angeles, California, October, 2011.

Coburn, W. J. (2011b) 'A warrior's stance: Commentary on paper by Terry Marks-Tarlow,' *Psychoanalytic Dialogues* 21: 128–139.

Coburn, W. J. (2012) 'Search yourself: Commentary on paper by Kenneth Frank,' *Psychoanalytic Dialogues* 22, 3: 328–340.

Coburn, W. J. and Frie, R. (Eds) (2010) *Persons in Context: The Challenge of Individuality in Theory and Practice,* New York: Routledge.

Coburn, W. J. and Shane, E. (2002a) 'Epilogue,' *Psychoanalytic Inquiry* 22, 5: 871–872..

Coburn, W. J. and Shane, E. (2002b) 'Prologue,' *Psychoanalytic Inquiry* 22, 5: 653–654.

Coburn, W. J. and Shane, E. (2008) 'Recognizing recognition in self psychology,' *International Journal of Psychoanalytic Self Psychology* 3, 2: 153–157.

Coburn, W. J. and VanDerHeide, N. (2009a) 'Introduction.' In W. J. Coburn and N. VanDerHeide (Eds.), *Self and Systems: Explorations in Contemporary Self Psychology,* Boston, MA: Blackwell Publishing on behalf of the Annals of the New York Academy of Sciences.

Coburn, W. J. and Shane, E. (Eds) (2009b) *Self and Systems: Explorations In Contemporary Self Psychology.* Boston, MA: Blackwell Publishing on behalf of the Annals of the New York Academy of Sciences.

Cooper, S. H. (1996) 'Facts all come with a point of view,' *International Journal of Psychoanalysis* 77, 2: 255–273.

Cooper, S. H. (2004) 'State of the hope: The new bad object in the therapeutic action of psychoanalysis,' *Psychoanalytic Dialogues* 14: 527–551.

Cover, T. M. and Thomas, J. A. (2006) *Elements of Information Theory* (2nd ed.), Hoboken, NJ: Wiley-Interscience.

Cushman, P. (1994) 'Confronting Sullivan's spider: Hermeneutics and the politics of therapy,' *Contemporary Psychoanalysis* 30: 800–844.

Cushman, P. (2011). 'So who's asking: Politics, hermeneutics, and individuality.' In R. Frie & W. J. Coburn (Eds.), *Persons in Context: The Challenge of Individuality in Theory and Practice,* New York: Routledge.

Davies, J. M. (2003) 'Falling in love with love: Oedipal and postoedipal manifestations of idealization, mourning, and erotic masochism,' *Psychoanalytic Dialogues* 13: 1–27.

Davies, J. M. (2004) 'Whose bad objects are we anyway? Repetition and our elusive love affair with evil,' *Psychoanalytic Dialogues* 14, 6: 711–732.

Davies, J. M. (2005) 'Transformations of desire and despair: Reflections on the termination process from a relational perspective,' *Psychoanalytic Dialogues* 15: 779–805.

Derrida, J. (1978) *Writing and Difference*, Chicago, IL: University of Chicago Press.

Dubois, P. (2003) 'Perturbing a dynamic order: Dynamic systems theory and clinical application,' Pre-published paper.

Dysart, D. (1977) 'Transference cure and narcissism,' *Journal of the American Academy of Psychoanalysis and Dynamic Psychiatry* 5: 17–29.

Eagle, M. (2003) 'The postmodern turn in psychoanalysis: A critique,' *Psychoanalytic Psychology* 20: 411–424.

Edelman, G. (1992) *Bright Air, Brilliant Fire*, New York: Basic Books.

Ehrenberg, D. B. (1992) *The Intimate Edge: Extending the Reach of Psychoanalytic Interaction*, New York: W. W. Norton.

Einstein, A. (1949) 'Autobiographical note.' In P. A. Schilpp (Ed.), *Albert Einstein: Philosopher–Scientist*. Evanston, Ill.: Open Court.

Emde, R. N. (1988) 'Development terminable and interminable: I. Innate and motivational factors from infancy.' *International Journal of Psycho-Analysis* 69: 23–42.

English, O. S. and Pearson, H. J. (1937) *Common Neuroses of Children and Adults*, New York: Norton.

Epstein, L. and Feiner, A. H. (1979) 'Countertransference: the therapist's contribution to treatment,' *Contemporary Psychoanalysis* 15, 3: 489–513.

Fairburn, W. D. (1958) 'On the nature and aims of psycho-analytical treatment,' *International Journal of Psycho-Analysis*, 39: 374–385.

Falk, D. (2012) Could the Internet ever "wake up?" *Slate: Future Tense*. Retrieved from http://www.slate.com/articles/technology/future_tense/2012/09/christof_koch_robert_sawyer_could_the_internet_ever_become_conscious_.single.html

Ferenczi, S. (1928) 'The elasticity of psycho-analytic technique.' In S. Ferenczi (Ed.), *Final Contributions to the Problems and Methods of Psycho-Analysis*, New York: Brunner/Mazel.

Ferenczi, S. (1955) *Final Contributions to the Problems and Methods of Psychoanalysis*, New York: Basic Books.

Field, N. (1991) 'Projective identification: mechanism or mystery?' *Journal of Analytic Psychology* 36: 93–109.

Fliess, R. (1942) 'The metapsychology of the analyst,' *Psychoanalytic Quarterly* 11: 211–227.

Fonagy, P. and Target, M. (1996) 'Playing with reality: I. Theory of mind and the normal development of psychic reality,' *International Journal of Psycho-Analysis* 77: 217–233.

Fonagy, P., Gergely, G., Jurist, E., and Target, M. (2002) *Affect Regulation, Mentalization and the Development of the Self*, New York: Other Books.

Fosshage, J. L. (1992) 'Self psychology: The self and its vicissitudes within a relational matrix.' In N. J. Skolnick and S. C. Warshaw (Eds.), *Relational Perspectives in Psychoanalysis*, Hillsdale, NJ: Analytic Press.

Fosshage, J. L. (1995) 'Toward a model of psychoanalytic supervision from a self psychological/intersubjective perspective.' In M. Rock (Ed.), *Psychodynamic Supervision: Issues for the Supervisor and Supervisee*, Northvale, NJ: Jason Aronson.

Fosshage, J. L. (2003) 'Contextualizing self psychology and relational psychoanalysis: Bi-directional influence and proposed syntheses,' *Contemporary Psychoanalysis* 39: 411–448.

Fosshage, J. L. (2005) 'The explicit and implicit domains in psychoanalytic change,' *Psychoanalytic Inquiry* 25: 516–539.

Foucault, M. (1977) *Discipline and Punish: The Birth of the Prison*, trans. A. Sheridan, London, UK: Allen Lane, Penguin.

Frank, K. A. (1997) 'The role of the analyst's inadvertent self-revelations,' *Psychoanalytic Dialogues* 7: 281–314.

Frank, K. A. (2012) 'Strangers to ourselves: Exploring the limits and potentials of the analyst's self awareness in self- and mutual analysis,' *Psychoanalytic Dialogues* 22: 311–327.

Freeman, W. J. (1995) *Society of Brains: A Study in the Neuroscience of Love and Hate*, Hillsdale, NJ: Lawrence Erlbaum Associates.

Freud, A. (1976) 'Changes in Psychoanalytic Practice and Experience,' *International Journal of Psycho-Analysis* 57: 257–260.

Freud, S. (1893) 'The psychotherapy of hysteria from studies on hysteria.' In J. Strachey (Ed. and trans.), *The Standard Edition of the Complete Psychological Works of Sigmund Freud* (vol. 2), New York: W. W. Norton.

Freud, S. (1910a) 'The future prospects of psycho-analytic therapy.' In J. Strachey (Ed. and trans.), *The Standard Edition of the Complete Psychological Works of Sigmund Freud* (vol. 11), New York: W. W. Norton.

Freud, S. (1910b) '"Wild" psycho-analysis.' In J. Strachey (Ed. and trans.), *The Standard Edition of the Complete Psychological Works of Sigmund Freud* (vol. 1), New York: W. W. Norton.

Freud, S. (1912) 'Recommendations to physicians practising psycho-analysis.' In J. Strachey (Ed. and trans.), *The Standard Edition of the Complete Psychological Works of Sigmund Freud* (vol. 12), New York: W. W. Norton.

Freud, S. (1913a) 'The disposition to obsessional neurosis.' In J. Strachey (Ed. and trans.), *The Standard Edition of the Complete Psychological Works of Sigmund Freud* (vol. 12), New York: W. W. Norton.

Freud, S. (1913b) 'On beginning the treatment (further recommendations on the technique of psycho-analysis I).' In J. Strachey (Ed. and trans.), *The Standard Edition of the Complete Psychological Works of Sigmund Freud* (vol. 12), New York: W. W. Norton.

Freud, S. (1914) 'Observations on transference-love.' In J. Strachey (Ed. and trans.), *The Standard Edition of the Complete Psychological Works of Sigmund Freud* (vol. 12), New York: W. W. Norton.

Freud, S. (1919) 'Lines of advance in psycho-analytic therapy.' In J. Strachey (Ed. and trans.), *The Standard Edition of the Complete Psychological Works of Sigmund Freud* (vol. 17), New York: W. W. Norton.

Freud, S. (1933) 'New introductory lectures on psycho-analysis.' In J. Strachey (Ed. and trans.), *The Standard Edition of the Complete Psychological Works of Sigmund Freud* (vol. 22), New York: W. W. Norton.

Freud, S. (1937) 'Analysis terminable and interminable.' In J. Strachey (Ed. and trans.), *The Standard Edition of the Complete Psychological Works of Sigmund Freud* (vol. 23), New York: W. W. Norton.

Freud, S. (1981a) 'Analysis terminable and interminable.' In J. Strachey (Ed. and trans.), *The Standard Edition of the Complete Psychological Works of Sigmund Freud* (vol. 23). London, UK: Hogarth. (Original work published 1937)

Freud, S. (1981b) 'The disposition to obsessional neurosis.' In J. Strachey (Ed. and trans.), *The Standard Edition of the Complete Psychological Works of Sigmund Freud* (vol. 12). London, UK: Hogarth. (Original work published 1913)

Freud, S. (1981c) 'The future prospects of psycho-analytic therapy.' In J. Strachey (Ed. and trans.), *The Standard Edition of the Complete Psychological Works of Sigmund Freud* (vol. 11). London: Hogarth. (Original work published 1910)

Freud, S. (1981d) 'Recommendations to physicians practising psycho-analysis.' In J. Strachey (Ed and trans.), *The Standard Edition of the Complete Psychological Works of Sigmund Freud* (vol. 12). London, UK: Hogarth. (Original work published 1912)

Frie, R. (1997) *Subjectivity and Intersubjectivity in Modern Philosophy and Psychoanalysis*, New York: Rowman and Littlefield.

Frie, R. (2003) 'Introduction: Between modernism and postmodernism: rethinking psychological agency.' In R. Frie (Ed.), *Understanding Experience: Psychotherapy and Postmodernism*, New York: Routledge.

Frie, R. (2010) 'Compassion, dialogue, and context: On understanding the other,' *International Journal of Psychoanalytic Self Psychology* 5: 451–466.

Frie, R. (2011) 'Culture and context: From individualism to situated experience,' In R. Frie and W. J. Coburn (Eds.), *Persons in Context: The Challenge of Individuality in Theory and Practice,* New York: Routledge.

Frie, R. and Coburn, W. J. (2011) *Persons in Context: The Challenge of Individuality in Theory and Practice*, New York: Routledge.

Frie, R. and Orange, D. (eds.) *Beyond Postmodernism: New Dimensions in Clinical Theory and Practice*, New York: Routledge.

Friedman, L. (1978) 'Trends in the psychoanalytic theory of treatment,' *The Psychoanalytic Quarterly* 47: 524–567.

Friedman, L. (1982) 'The humanistic trend in recent psychoanalytic theory,' *Psychoanalytic Quarterly* 51: 353–371.

Friedman, L. (1988) *The Anatomy of Psychotherapy*, Hillsdale, NJ: The Analytic Press.

Friedman, L. (2005) 'Psychoanalytic treatment: Thick soup or thin gruel?' *Psychoanalytic Inquiry* 25: 418–439.

Gabbard, G. O. and Westen, D. (2003) 'Rethinking therapeutic action,' *International Journal of Psycho-Analysis* 84: 823–841.

Gadamer, H.-G. (1991) *Truth and Method*, 2nd ed., trans. J. Weinsheimer and D. Marshall, New York: Crossroad.

Galatzer-Levy, R. (1978) 'Qualitative change from quantitative change: Mathematical catastrophe theory in relation to psychoanalysis,' *Journal of the American Psychoanalytic Association* 26: 921–935.

Gedo, J. (1999) *The Evolution of Psychoanalysis*, New York: Other Press.

Gell-Mann, M. (1994) *The Quark and the Jaguar: Adventures in the Simple and the Complex*, New York: W. H. Freeman.

Gentile, J. (2007) 'Wrestling with matter: Origins of intersubjectivity,' *Psychoanalytic Quarterly* 76: 547–582.

Gentile, J. (2008) 'Between private and public: Towards a conception of the transitional subject,' *International Journal of Psycho-Analysis* 89: 959–976.

Gentile, J. (2010) 'Weeds on the ruins: Agency, compromise formation, and the quest for intersubjective truth,' *Psychoanalytic Dialogues* 20: 88–109.

Ghent, E. (1990) 'Masochism, submission, surrender—masochism as a perversion of surrender,' *Contemporary Psychoanalysis* 26: 108–136.

Ghent, E. (2002) 'Wish, need, drive,' *Psychoanalytic Dialogues* 12: 763–808.

Gill, M. (1983) 'The interpersonal paradigm and the degree of the therapist's involvement,' *Contemporary Psychoanalysis* 19, 2: 202–237.

Gill, M. (1984) 'Transference: A change in conception or only in emphasis?' *Psychoanalytic Inquiry* 4: 489–523.

Glover, E. (1937) 'Symposium on the theory of the therapeutic results of psycho-analysis,' *International Journal of Psycho-Analysis* 18: 125–189.

Godwin, R. (1991) 'Wilfred Bion and David Bohm: Toward a quantum metapsychology,' *Psychoanalysis and Contemporary Thought* 14, 4: 625–654.

Goldberg, A. L. and Rigney, D. R. (1998) 'Sudden death is not chaos.' In S. Krasner (Ed.), *The Ubiquity of Chaos*, Washington, DC: American Association for the Advancement of Science.

Goldstein, J. (1996) 'Causality and emergence in chaos and complexity theories.' In W. Sulis (Ed.), *Nonlinear Dynamics and Human Behavior*, Singapore: World Scientific Publishing.

Greenberg, J. R. (1981) 'Prescription or description: The therapeutic action of psychoanalysis,' *Contemporary Psychoanalysis* 17: 239–257.

Grinberg, L. (1962) 'On a specific aspect of countertransference due to the patient's projective identification,' *International Journal of Psycho-Analysis* 43: 436–440.

Grotstein, J. S. (1977) *Splitting and Projective Identification*, New York: Jason Aronson.

Grotstein, J. S. (1995) 'Projective identification reappraised—projective identification, introjective identification, the transference/countertransference neurosis/psychosis, and their consummate expression in the crucifixion, the pietà, and "therapeutic Exorcism," part II: The countertransference complex,' *Contemporary Psychoanalysis* 31: 479–511.

Grotstein, J. S. (2007) 'On: projective identification,' *International Journal of Psycho-Analysis* 88: 1289–1290.

Grotstein, J. S. (2009a) *But at the Same Time and on Another Level: Vol. 1: Psychoanalytic Theory and Technique in the Kleinian/Bionian Mode*, London, UK: Karnac Books.

Grotstein, J. S. (2009b) *But at the Same Time and on Another Level: Vol. 2: Clinical Applications in the Kleinian/Bionian Mode,* London, UK: Karnac Books.

Hacking, I. (1999) *The Social Construction of What?* Cambridge, MA: Harvard University Press.

Harris, J. F. (1992) *Against Relativism: A Philosophical Defense of Method*, La Salle, IL: Open Court.

Harris, A. (2005) *Gender as Soft Assembly*, Hillsdale, NJ: Analytic Press.

Heidegger, M. (1962) *Being and Time*, trans. J. Macquarrie and E. Robinson, New York: Harper and Row. (Original work published 1927)

Heimann, P. (1950) 'On countertransference,' *International Journal of Psycho-Analysis* 31: 81–84.

Heisenberg, W. (1958) *Physics and Philosophy: The Revolution in Modern Science,* New York: Harper and Row.

Hinshelwood, R. D. (1982) 'Review of "Living Groups: Group Psychotherapy and General System Theory,"' *International Journal of Psycho-Analysis* 63: 497–500.

Hoffman, I. Z. (1994) 'Dialectical thinking and therapeutic action in the psychoanalytic process,' *Psychoanalytic Quarterly* 63: 187–218.

Hoffman, I. Z. (1998) *Ritual and Spontaneity in the Psychoanalytic Process: A Dialectical-Constructivist View,* New York: Routledge.

Hoffman, I. Z. (2009) 'Therapeutic passion in the countertransference,' *Psychoanalytic Dialogues* 19: 617–637.

Holt, J. (2012) *Why Does the World Exist? An Existential Detective Story*, New York: Liveright.

James, H. (1881, 2008) *The Portrait of a Lady*, Volume 1 (of 2), Gutenberg EBook #2833, Produced by Eve Sobol and David Widger, Project Gutenberg.

Kauffman, S. A. (1995) *At Home in the Universe: The Search for Laws of Self-Organization and Complexity*, New York: Oxford University Press.

Keats, J. (1899) *The Complete Poetical Works and Letters of John Keats, Cambridge ed.* Boston, MA: Houghton, Mifflin and Company.

Kellert, S. H. (1993) *In the Wake of Chaos*, Chicago, IL: University of Chicago Press.

Kelso, J. A. S. (1995) *Dynamic Patterns: The Self-organization of Brain and Behavior*, Cambridge, MA: MIT Press.

Kepes, G. (1965) *Structure in Art and Science*, New York: Vision and Values Series.

Kernberg, O. F. (1976) *Object Relations Theory and Clinical Psychoanalysis*. New York: Jason Aronson.

Kernberg, O. F. (1984) *Severe Personality Disorders: Psychotherapeutic Strategies*, New Haven, CT: Yale University Press.

Kernberg, O. F. (1987) 'Projection and projective identification: Developmental and clinical aspects,' *Journal of the American Psychoanalytic Association* 35: 795–819.

Klein, M. (1946) 'Notes on some schizoid mechanisms,' *International Journal of Psycho-Analysis* 27: 99–110.

Knoblauch, S. (2000) *The Musical Edge of Therapeutic Dialogue*, Hillsdale, NJ: The Analytic Press.

Kohut, H. (1959) 'Introspection, empathy, and psychoanalysis—an examination of the relationship between mode of observation and theory,' *Journal of the American Psychoanalytic Association* 7: 459–483.

Kohut, H. (1971) *The Analysis of the Self*, Madison, CT: International Universities Press.

Kohut, H. (1977) *The Restoration of the Self*, New York: International Universities Press.

Kohut, H. (1982) Introspection, empathy, and the semi-circle of mental health: An examination of the relationship between mode of observation and theory. *International Journal of Psycho-Analysis* 63: 395–407.

Kohut, H. (1984) *How Does Analysis Cure?* Chicago, IL: University of Chicago Press.

Krakauer, D. (2009) *Complex Adaptive Systems and Childish Wonder: A Conversation with David Krakauer*. Retrieved from http://thesciencenetwork.org/programs/ santa-fe-institute-2009/david-krakauer

Kuhn, T. S. (1962) *The Structure of Scientific Revolutions* (3rd ed.), Chicago, IL: University of Chicago Press.

Lachmann, F. M. (2000) *Transforming Aggression: Psychotherapy with the Difficult-to-Treat Patient*, Northvale, NJ: Jason Aronson.

Lachmann, F. M. (2008) *Transforming Narcissism: Reflections on Empathy, Humor, and Expectations*, Northvale, NJ: Jason Aronson.

Laszlo, E. (1972) *Introduction to Systems Philosophy: Toward a New Paradigm of Contemporary Thought*, New York: Gordon and Breach, Science Publishers.

Lear, J. (2007) 'Working through the end of civilization,' *International Journal of Psycho-Analysis* 88: 291–308.

Levenson, E. A. (2003) 'On seeing what is said: Visual aids to the psychoanalytic process,' *Contemporary Psychoanalysis* 39: 233–249.

Lichtenberg, J. (2008) 'The (and this) analyst's intentions,' *Psychoanalytic Review* 95, 711–727.

Lichtenberg, J. D., Lachmann, F. M., and Fosshage, J. L. (1992) *Self and Motivational Systems: Toward a Theory of Psychoanalytic Technique*, Hillsdale, NJ: Analytic Press.

Lichtenberg, J. D., Lachmann, F. M., and Fosshage, J. L. (1996) *The Clinical Exchange: Techniques Derived from Self and Motivational Systems*, Hillsdale, NJ: The Analytic Press.

Lichtenberg, J. D., Lachmann, F. M., and Fosshage, J. L. (2002) *A Spirit of Inquiry: Communication in Psychoanalysis*, Hillsdale, NJ: The Analytic Press.

Lichtenberg, J. D., Lachmann, F. M., and Fosshage, J. L. (2011) *Psychoanalysis and Motivational Systems: A New Look*, New York: Routledge.

Little, M. (1951) 'Countertransference and the patient's response to it,' *International Journal of Psycho-Analysis* 32: 32–40.

Loewald, H. W. (1960) 'On the therapeutic action of psycho-analysis,' *The International Journal of Psychoanalysis* 41: 16–33.

Loewald, H. W. (1972) 'The experience of time,' *Psychoanalytic Study of the Child* 27: 401–410.

Lorenz, E. N. (1963, March) 'Deterministic nonperiodic flow,' *Journal of the Atmospheric Sciences* 20, 2: 130–141.

Lorenz, E. N. (1993) *The Essence of Chaos*, Seattle, WA: University of Washington Press.

Lyons-Ruth, K. (1999) 'The two-person unconscious: Intersubjective dialogue, enactive relational representation, and the emergence of new forms of relational organization,' *Psychoanalytic Inquiry*, 19: 576–617.

Lyotard, J. F. (1984) *The Postmodern Condition: A Report on Knowledge*, Minneapolis, MN: University of Minnesota Press.

Magid, B. (2002) *Ordinary Mind: Exploring the Common Ground of Zen and Psychotherapy*, Boston, MA: Wisdom.

Main, M. (1993) 'Discourse, prediction, and recent studies in attachment: Implications for psychoanalysis,' *Journal of the American Psychoanalytic Association* 41S: 209–244.

Main, M., Kaplan, N., and Cassidy, J. (1985) 'Security in infancy, childhood, and adulthood: A move to the level of representation,' *Monographs of the Society for Research in Child Development* 50: 66–104.

Malin, A. (1966) 'Projective identification in the therapeutic process,' *International Journal of Psycho-Analysis* 47: 26–31.

Mandel, A. J. and Selz, K. A. (1996) 'Nonlinear dynamical patterns as personality theory for neurobiology and psychoanalysis,' *Psychiatry* 58: 371–390.

Mandelbrot, B. B. (1982) *The Fractal Geometry of Nature*, San Francisco, CA: W. H. Freeman.

Marks-Tarlow, T. (2011) 'Merging and emerging: A nonlinear portrait of intersubjectivity during psychotherapy,' *Psychoanalytic Dialogues* 21: 110–127.

Masler, D. (forthcoming) 'The self of the field and the work of Donnel Stern,' PsyD dissertation, Antioch University.

Mayer, E. L. (1996) 'Subjectivity and intersubjectivity of clinical facts,' *International Journal of Psycho-Analysis* 77: 707–737.

Mead, M. (1942) *And Keep Your Powder Dry: An Anthropologist Looks at America*, New York: Morrow.

Mendelsohn, R. (2011) 'Projective identification and countertransference in borderline couples,' *Psychoanalytic Review*, 98: 375–399.

Merleau-Ponty, M. (1968) *The Visible and the Invisible*, trans. A. Lingis, Evanston, IL: Northwestern University Press.

Merleau-Ponty, M. (2002) *Phenomenology of Perception,* trans. C. Smith, London, UK: Routledge. (Original work published 1945)

Miller, M. L. (1999) 'Chaos, complexity and psychoanalysis,' *Psychoanalytic Psychology* 16: 355–379.

Mills, J. (2000) 'Hegel on projective identification: Implications for Klein, Bion, and beyond,' *Psychoanalytic Review* 87: 841–874.

Mitchell, S. A. (1988) 'Relational Concepts in Psychoanalysis: An Integration,' Cambridge, MA: Harvard University Press.

Mitchell, S. A. (1993) *Hope and Dread in Psychoanalysis*, New York: Basic Books.

Mitchell, S. A. (1996) 'Introduction,' *Psychoanalytic Dialogues*, 6: 151–153.

Mitchell, S. A. (1997) *Influence and Autonomy in Psychoanalysis*, Hillsdale, NJ: The Analytic Press.

Mitchell, S. A. (2000) *Relationality: From Attachment to Intersubjectivity*, Hillsdale, NJ: The Analytic Press.

Mollon, P. (1989) 'Anxiety, supervision and a space for thinking: Some narcissistic perils for clinical psychologists in learning psychotherapy,' *British Journal of Medical Psychology* 62: 113–122.

Molnar, F. (2005) *The Paul Street Boys*, trans. L. Rittenberg, Budapest: Corvina. (Original work published 1906).

Monty Python's Life of Brian. (1979) motion picture, HandMade Films, distributed by Warner Bros., USA.

Moran, M. G. (1991) 'Chaos theory and psychoanalysis: The fluidic nature of the mind,' *International Review of Psycho-Analysis* 18: 211–221.

Nabokov, V. (1955) *Lolita*, New York: Berkley Medallion Books.

Nagel, T. (1986) *The View from Nowhere*, Oxford, UK: Oxford University Press.

Ogden, T. H. (1979) 'On projective identification,' *International Journal of Psycho-Analysis* 60: 357–373.

Ogden, T. H. (1994) 'The analytic third: working with intersubjective clinical facts,' *International Journal of Psycho-Analysis* 75: 3–19.

Orange, D. M. (1992) 'Subjectivism, relativism, and realism in psychoanalysis,' *Progress in Self Psychology* 8: 189–197.

Orange, D. M. (1993) 'Countertransference, empathy, and the hermeneutical circle.' In A. Goldberg (Ed.), *The Widening Scope of Self Psychology*, Hillsdale, NJ: Analytic Press.

Orange, D. M. (1995) *Emotional Understanding: Studies in Psychoanalytic Epistemology*, New York: Guilford Press.

Orange, D. M. (2001) 'From Cartesian minds to experiential worlds in psychoanalysis,' *Psychoanalytic Psychology* 18: 287–302.

Orange, D. M. (2002) 'There is no outside: Empathy and authenticity in psychoanalytic process,' *Psychoanalytic Psychology* 19: 686–700.

Orange, D. M. (2003a) 'Antidotes and alternatives: Perspectival realism and the new reductionisms,' *Psychoanalytic Psychology* 20: 472–486.

Orange, D. M. (2003b) 'Why language matters to psychoanalysis,' *Psychoanalytic Dialogues* 13, 1: 77–103.

Orange, D. M. (2006) 'For whom the bell tolls: Context, complexity, and compassion in psychoanalysis,' *International Journal of Psychoanalytic Self Psychology* 1, 1: 5–22.

Orange, D. M. (2008) 'Recognition as: Intersubjective vulnerability in the psychoanalytic dialogue,' *International Journal of Psychoanalytic Self Psychology* 3: 178–194.

Orange, D. M. (2009) 'Kohut memorial lecture: attitudes, values and intersubjective vulnerability,' *International Journal of Psychoanalytic Self Psychology* 4, 2: 235–253.

Orange, D. M. (2011) *The Suffering Stranger: Hermeneutics for Everyday Clinical Practice*, New York: Routledge/Taylor and Francis.

Orange, D. M., Atwood, G. E., and Stolorow, R. D. (1997) *Working Intersubjectively: Contextualism In Psychoanalytic Practice*, Hillsdale, NJ: Analytic Press.

Orr, D. (1954) 'Transference and countertransference: A historical survey,' *Journal of the American Psychoanalytic Association* 2: 621–670.

Palombo, S. R. (1999) *The Emergent Ego: Complexity and Coevolution in the Psychoanalytic Process*. Madison, CT: International Universities Press.

Percus, A., Istrate, G., and Moore, C. (Eds.) (2005) *Computational Complexity and Statistical Physics*, New York: Oxford University Press.

Phillips, A. (1998) *The Beast in the Nursery: On Curiosity and Other Appetites*, New York: Vintage.

Phillips, A. (1999) *Darwin's Worms: On Life Stories and Death Stories,* New York: Vintage.

Pickles, J. (2006) 'A systems sensibility: commentary on Judith Teicholz's "Qualities of Engagement and the Analyst's Theory,"' *International Journal of Psychoanalytic Self Psychology* 1, 3: 301–316.

Pickles, J. and Coburn, W. (2008) 'Introduction,' *International Journal of Psychoanalytic Self Psychology* 3, 1: 125.

Piers, C. (2000) 'Character as self-organizing complexity,' *Psychoanalysis and Contemporary Thought* 23: 3–34.

Piers, C. (2005) 'The mind's multiplicity and continuity,' *Psychoanalytic Dialogues* 15, 2: 229–254.

Pizer, S. A. (1996) 'The distributed self: Introduction to symposium On "The Multiplicity of Self and Analytic Technique,"' *Contemporary Psychoanalysis* 32: 499–507.

Pizer, S. A. (1998) *Building Bridges: The Negotiation of Paradox in Psychoanalysis,* New York: Routledge.

Poincaré, L. and Guillaume, C. É. (1900) *Rapports Présentés au Congrès International de Physique Réuni à Paris en 1900 sous les Auspices de la Société Française de Physique.* Paris, Gauthier-Villars.

Preston, L. (2008) 'The edge of awareness: Gendlin's contribution to explorations of implicit experience,' *International Journal of Psychoanalytic Self Psychology* 3: 347–369.

Prigogine, I. (1996) *The End of Certainty*, New York: Free Press.

Prigogine, I. and J. Holte (1993) *Chaos: The New Science* (Nobel Conference XXVI). St. Peter, MN: Gustavus Adolphus College.

Proust, M. (2003) *Swann's Way*, New York: Viking Penguin

Rabin, H. M. (1995) 'The liberating effect on the analyst of the paradigm shift in psychoanalysis,' *Psychoanalytic Psychology* 12: 467–481.

Racker, H. (1968) *Transference and Counter-transference*, New York: International Universities Press.

Ramsey, F. P. (1990) *Philosophical Papers*, ed. D. H. Mellor, Cambridge, UK: Cambridge University Press.

Reich, W. (1945) *Character Analysis* (3rd ed.), New York: Simon and Schuster.

Reik, T. (1948) 'The surprised psychoanalyst.' In B. Wolstein (Ed.), *Essential Papers on Countertransference*, New York: New York University Press.

Renik, O. (1980) 'International Journal of Psychoanalytic Psychotherapy, VII, 1978–1979: Projective identification and maternal impingement, Darius Ornston, pp. 508–532' *Psychoanalytic Quarterly* 49: 551–552.

Ricci, M., Trigault, N., et al. (1622) *Entrata nella China de' della Compagnia del Gesv.* Naples: Lazzaro Scoriggio.

Ringstrom, P. A. (2001) 'Cultivating the improvisational in psychoanalytic treatment,' *Psychoanalytic Dialogues* 11: 727–754.

Rumelhart, D. and McClelland, J. (1986) *Parallel Distributed Processing: Explorations in the Microstructure of Cognition* (vol. 1), Cambridge, MA: MIT Press.

Russell, B. (1966) 'The Philosophy of Logical Atomism'. In R. C. Marsh (ed.), *Logic and Knowledge: Essays 1901–1950*. London: George Allen & Unwin Ltd. (Original work published 1918).

Sander, L. W. (1977) 'The regulation of exchange in the infant–caretaker system and some aspects of the context–content relationship.' In M. Lewis and L. Rosenblum (Eds.), *Interaction, Conversation, and the Development of Language*, New York: Wiley.

Sander, L. W. (1985) 'Toward a logic of organization in psychobiological development.' In K. Klar and L. Siever (Eds.), *Biologic Response Styles: Clinical Implications*, Washington, DC: American Psychiatric Press.

Sander, L. W. (1992) 'Countertransference,' *International Journal of Psycho-Analysis* 73: 582–584.

Sander, L. W. (2002) 'Thinking differently,' *Psychoanalytic Dialogues* 12: 11–42.

Sander, L. W. (1988) 'The event-structure of regulation in the neonate-caregiver system as a biological background for early organization of psychic structure,' *Progress in Self Psychology* 3: 64–77.

Sandler, J. (1976) 'Countertransference and role-responsiveness,' *International Review of Psycho-Analysis* 3: 43–47.

Sands, S. (1997) 'Self psychology and projective identification—wither shall they meet?' *Psychoanalytic Dialogues* 7, 5: 651–668.

Sartre, J.-P. (1948) *Being and Nothingness*, trans. H. E. Barnes, New York: Philosophical Library.

Sashin, J. I. and Callahan, J. (1990) 'A model of affect using dynamical systems,' *Annual of Psychoanalysis* 18: 213–231.

Schafer, R. (1983) *The Analytic Attitude*, New York: Basic Books.

Scharff, D. E. (2000) 'Fairbairn and the self as an organized system,' *Canadian Journal of Psychoanalysis* 8: 181–195.

Searle, J. R. and Vanderveken, D. (1985) *Foundations of Illocutionary Logic*, Cambridge, UK: Cambridge University Press.

Searles, H. F. (1965) *Collected Papers on Schizophrenia and Related Subjects*, New York: International Universities Press.

Searles, H. F. (1979) *Countertransference and Related Subjects*, New York: International Universities Press.

Seligman, S. (1999) 'Integrating Kleinian theory and intersubjective infant research: Observing projective identification,' *Psychoanalytic Dialogues* 9: 129–159.

Seligman, S. (2005) 'Dynamic systems theories as a metaframework for psychoanalysis,' *Psychoanalytic Dialogues* 15, 2: 285–319.

Seligman, S. (2012) 'The baby out of the bathwater: Microseconds, psychic structure, and psychotherapy,' *Psychoanalytic Dialogues* 22: 499–509.

Seligman, S. and Shanok, R.S. (1995) 'Subjectivity, complexity and the social world: Erikson's identity concept and contemporary relational theories,' *Psychoanalytic Dialogues* 5: 537–565.

Shane, E. (2006) 'Developmental systems self psychology,' *International Journal of Psychoanalytic Self Psychology* 1: 23–45.

Shane, E. (2007) How does analysis cure? Understanding the complexities of the therapeutic process through pluralistic dialogue: an integrative overview and summary of "Finding Renee (A Clinical Symposium in Four Parts),"' *International Journal of Psychoanalytic Self Psychology* 2: 131–146.

Shane E. & Carlton, L. (2009). *From the Bottom up: How a Brain-Based Psychoanalytic Theory Contributes to Relational Understanding of Memory*. Paper delivered at the 2009 Annual IARPP Conference, Tel Aviv, Israel.

Shane, E. and Coburn, W. J. (2002) 'Prologue,' *Psychoanalytic Inquiry* 22: 653–654.

Shane, M., Shane, E. and Gales, M. (1997) *Intimate Attachments: Toward a New Self Psychology*, New York: Guilford.

Shapiro, D. (2000) *Dynamics of Character*, New York: Basic Books.

Slavin, M. O. (1996) 'Is one self enough? Multiplicity in self-organization and the capacity to negotiate relational conflict,' *Contemporary Psychoanalysis* 32: 615–625.

Slochower, J. (1996) 'Holding and the fate of the analyst's subjectivity,' *Psychoanalytic Dialogues* 6: 323–353.

Sperry, M. (2011) 'This better be good! complex systems and the dread of influence,' *International Journal of Psychoanalytic Self Psychology* 6: 74–98.

Spruiell, V. (1993) 'Deterministic chaos and the sciences of complexity: Psychoanalysis in the midst of a general scientific revolution,' *Journal of the American Psychoanalytic Association* 41: 3–44.

Steinberg, M. C. (2006) 'Language, the medium of change: The implicit in the talking cure,' Pre-published paper.

Stern, A. (1924) 'On the counter-transference in psychoanalysis,' *Psychoanalytic Review* 11: 166–174.

Stern, D. B. (1997) *Unformulated Experience: From Dissociation to Imagination in Psychoanalysis*. Hillsdale, NJ: The Analytic Press.

Stern, D. B. (2012) 'Implicit theories of technique and the values that inspire them,' Psychoanalytic Inquiry, 32: 33–49.

Stern, D. N. (1985) *The Interpersonal World of the Infant*, New York: Basic Books.

Stern, D. N. (2004) *The Present Moment in Psychotherapy and Everyday Life*, New York: W. W. Norton.

Stern, D. N., Sander, L., Nahum, J., Harrison, A., Lyons-Ruth, K., Morgan, A., Bruschweilerstern, N., and Tronik, E. (1998) 'Non-interpretive mechanisms in psychoanalytic therapy: The 'something more' than interpretation,' *International Journal of Psychoanalysis* 79: 903–921.

Stolorow, R. D. (1994) 'The nature and therapeutic action of psychoanalytic interpretation.' In R. Stolorow. G. Atwood, and B. Brandchaft (Eds.), *The Intersubjective Perspective*, Northvale, NJ: Aronson.

Stolorow, R. D. (1995) 'An intersubjective view of self psychology,' *Psychoanalytic Dialogues* 5: 393–399.

Stolorow, R. D. (1997) 'Dynamic, dyadic, intersubjective systems: An evolving paradigm for psychoanalysis,' *Psychoanalytic Psychology* 14: 337–364.

Stolorow, R. D. (2007) *Trauma and Human Existence: Autobiographical, Psychoanalytic and Philosophical Reflections*, New York: The Analytic Press.

Stolorow, R. D. (2012, May 25) 'Ode to a Besserwisser,' [Web log post]. Retrieved from http://www.psychologytoday.com/blog/feeling-relating-existing/201205/ode-besserwisser

Stolorow, R. D. and Atwood, G. E. (1979) *Faces in a Cloud: Subjectivity in Personality Theory* (1st ed.). Northvale, NJ: Jason Aronson.

Stolorow, R. D. and Atwood, G. E. (1992) *Contexts of Being: The Intersubjective Foundations of Psychological Life*, Hillsdale, NJ: Analytic Press.

Stolorow, R. D. and Atwood, G. E. (1993) *Faces in a Cloud: Intersubjectivity in Personality Theory* (2nd ed.), Northvale, NJ: Jason Aronson.

Stolorow, R. D. and Atwood, G. E. (1996) 'The intersubjective perspective,' *Psychoanalytic Review* 83: 181–194.

Stolorow, R. D., Atwood, G. E., and Brandchaft, B. (Eds.) (1994) *The Intersubjective Perspective*, Northvale, NJ: Jason Aronson.

Stolorow, R. D., Atwood, G. E., and Orange, D. M. (1998) 'On psychoanalytic truth,' *International Journal of Psycho-Analysis* 79: 1221.

Stolorow, R. D., Atwood, G. E., and Orange, D. M. (2002) *Worlds of Experience: Interweaving Philosophical and Clinical Dimensions in Psychoanalysis*, New York: Basic Books.

Stolorow, R. D., Atwood, G. E., and Orange, D. M. (2010) 'Heidegger's Nazism and the hypostatization of being,' *International Journal of Psychoanalytic Self Psychology* 5: 429–450.

Stolorow, R. D., Brandchaft, B., and Atwood, G. E. (1987) *Psychoanalytic Treatment: An Intersubjective Approach*, Hillsdale, NJ: Analytic Press.

Stolorow, R. D. and Jacobs, L. (2006) 'Critical reflections on Husserl's phenomenological quest for purity: Implications for gestalt therapy,' *International Gestalt Journal* 29, 2: 43–61.

Stolorow, R. D. and Orange, D. M. (2003) 'Review of "Mistaken Identity: The Mind-Brain Problem Reconsidered" by Leslie Brothers,' *Psychoanalytic Quarterly* 72: 515–518.

Stolorow, R. D., Orange, D. M., and Atwood, G. E. (1998) 'Projective identification begone! Commentary on paper by Susan H. Sands,' *Psychoanalytic Dialogues* 8, 5: 719–725.

Stolorow, R. D., Orange, D. M., and Atwood, G. E. (2001a) 'Cartesian and post-Cartesian trends in relational psychoanalysis,' *Psychoanalytic Psychology* 18: 468–484.

Stolorow, R. D., Orange, D. M., and Atwood, G. E. (2001b) 'World horizons: A post-Cartesian alternative to the Freudian unconscious,' *Contemporary Psychoanalysis* 37: 43–61.

Strenger, C. (1998) 'The desire for self-creation,' *Psychoanalytic Dialogues* 8: 625–655.

Sucharov, M. S. (1994) 'Psychoanalysis, self psychology, and intersubjectivity.' In R. D. Stolorow, G. E. Atwood, and B. Brandchaft (Eds.), *The Intersubjective Perspective*, New York: Jason Aronson.

Sucharov, M. S. (2002) 'Representation and the intrapsychic: Cartesian barriers to empathic contact,' *Psychoanalytic Inquiry* 22, 5: 686–707.

Sullivan, H. S. (1940) *Conceptions in Modern Psychiatry*, New York: W. W. Norton.

Sullivan, H. S. (1962) *Schizophrenia As a Human Process*, New York: W. W. Norton.

Talking Heads. (1980) 'Once in a lifetime,' on *Remain in Light* [CD]. New York: Warner Bros.

Tansey, M. H. and Burke, W. F. (1985) 'Projective identification and the empathic process— interactional communications,' *Contemporary Psychoanalysis* 21: 42–69.

Taupin, B. and John, E. (1969) 'Your song,' on *Elton John* [CD]. New York: BMI.

Taylor, M. C. (2001) *The Moment of Complexity: Emerging Network Culture*, Chicago, IL: University of Chicago Press.

Thelen, E. (2005) 'Dynamic systems theory and the complexity of change,' *Psychoanalytic Dialogues* 15, 2: 255–283.

Thelen, E. and Smith, L. B. (1994) *A Dynamic Systems Approach to the Development of Cognition and Action*, Cambridge, MA: MIT Press.

Thom, R. (1974) *Modèles Mathématiques de la Morphogenèse: Recueil de Textes sur la Théorie des Catastrophes et ses Applications*, Paris: Union Général d'Éditions.

Thomson, P. (1991) 'Countertransference in an intersubjective perspective.' In A. Goldberg (Ed.), *The Evolution of Self Psychology*, New York: Analytic Press.

Tolpin, M. (2002) 'Doing psychoanalysis of normal development: Forward edge transferences,' *Progress in Self Psychology* 18: 167–190.

Tolpin, M. (2007) 'The divided self: Shifting an intrapsychic balance the forward edge of a kinship transference: To bleed like everyone else,' *Psychoanalytic Inquiry* 27: 50–65.

Tower, L. E. (1956) 'Countertransference,' *Journal of the American Psychoanalytic Association* 4: 224–255.

Trevarthen, C. (1979) 'Communication and cooperation in early infancy.' In M. Bullowa (Ed.), *Before Speech,* New York: Cambridge University Press.

Tronick, E. Z. (1989) 'Emotions and emotional communication infants,' *American Psychologist* 44: 112–119.

Trop, G., Burke, M., and Trop, J. (2000) 'Contextualism and dynamic systems in psychoanalysis: Rethinking the language of intersubjectivity theory.' Paper presented at the APA Division 39 (Psychoanalysis) Conference, Washington, DC, 2000.

Trop, G., Burke, M., and Trop, J. (2002) 'Thinking dynamically in psychoanalytic theory and practice,' *Progress In Self Psychology* 18: 129–147.

VanDerHeide, N. (2009) 'A dynamic systems view of the transformational process of mirroring,' *International Journal of Psychoanalytic Self Psychology* 4: 432–444.

VanDerHeide, N. (2011) 'The two-way mirror: Response to discussions by Hershberg and Philips,' *International Journal of Psychoanalytic Self Psychology* 6: 67–73.

Varela, F. J., Thompson, E., and Rosch, E. (1991) *The Embodied Mind: Cognitive Science and Human Experience,* Cambridge, MA: MIT Press.

von Bertalanffy, L. (1968) *General Systems Theory*, New York: Braziller.

von Foerster, H. (1981) *Observing Systems*, Seaside, CA: Intersystems.

Waddington, C. H. (1966) *Principles of Development and Differentiation*, New York: Macmillan.

Waddington, C. H. (1977) *Tools for Thought: How to Understand and Apply the Latest Scientific Techniques of Problem Solving*, New York: Basic Books.

Weiner, N. (1948) *Cybernetics: Or Control and Communication in the Animal and the Machine,* Cambridge, MA: Hermann and Cie.

Weisel-Barth, J. (2006) 'Thinking and writing about complexity theory in the clinical setting,' *International Journal of Psychoanalytic Self Psychology* 1, 4: 365–388.

Weiss, J. (1986) 'Unconscious guilt.' In J. Weiss and H. Sampson (Eds.), *The Psychoanalytic Process: Theory, Clinical Observation, and Empirical Research,* New York: Guilford

White, E. B. (1949) *Here Is New York*, New York: Harper & Bros.

Winnicott, D. W. (1949) 'Hate in the counter-transference,' *International Journal of Psycho-Analysis* 30: 69–74.

Winnicott, D. W. (1953) 'Transitional objects and transitional phenomena—a study of the first not-me possession,' *International Journal of Psycho-Analysis* 34: 89–97.

Winnicott, D. W. (1965) *The Maturational Processes and the Facilitating Environment: Studies in the Theory of Emotional Development*, Madison, CT: International Universities Press.

Winnicott, D. W. (1971) *Playing and Reality*, Middlesex, UK: Penguin.

Winnicott, D. W. (1986) *Holding and Interpretation: Fragment of An Analysis*, London, UK: The Hogarth Press and the Institute of Psycho-Analysis.

Wittgenstein, L. (2001) *Philosophical Investigations*, London, UK: Blackwell. (Original work published 1953)

Wolf, E. (1983) 'Empathy and counter-transference.' In A. Goldberg (Ed.), *The Future of Psychoanalysis*, New York: International Universities Press.

Wolf, E. (1996) 'The irrelevance of infant observations for psychoanalysis,' *Journal of the American Psychoanalytic Association* 44: 369–392.

Yglesias, R. (1996) *Dr. Neruda's Cure for Evil*, New York: Warner Books.

Index